MW00652772

A TREATISE ON
INTERIOR
PEACE

About the Editor: Sister Marie Celeste, SC is a Mother Seton Sister of Charity, a professor of Modern Languages and Literatures, and an international scholar and author. She holds a PhD in French Studies from Laval University, Quebec, certificates of study from the Sorbonne and *L'Institut Catholique* of Paris, from the University of Madrid, and from the University of Perugia, Italy. Her books and translations have been published in France, Canada and the United States. Her major French works embody studies on Georges Bernanos, Graham Greene and the famed Black-African author, Cheikh Hamidou Kane. She has authored several major works on Elizabeth Ann Seton based on the saint's own writings, namely, *A Self-Portrait; The Intimate Friendships; A Woman of Prayer.* She has won numerous awards in the United States and abroad and is listed in the *World's Who's Who of Women.*

A TREATISE ON INTERIOR PEACE

Reverend Ambroise de Lombez OFM, Cap

Translated by Saint Elizabeth Ann Seton

Edited by Sister Marie Celeste, SC

ALBA·HOUSE alba house NEW·YORK

SOCIETY OF ST. PAUL, 2187 VICTORY BLVD., STATEN ISLAND, NEW YORK 10314

Library of Congress Cataloging-in-Publication Data

Ambroise de Lombez, pere, 1708-1778.
  [Traité de la paix intérieure. English]
  A treatise on interior peace / Ambroise de Lombez; translated
into English by Saint Elizabeth Ann Seton; edited by Sister Marie
Celeste, SC.
        p.   cm.
  Includes bibliographical references.
  ISBN 0-8189-0715-0
  1. Spiritual life — Catholic authors.   I. Marie Celeste, Sister,
S.C.   II. Title.
BX2350.2.A4413   1996
248.4'82 — dc20   95-45564
                                                   CIP

Produced and designed in the United States of America by the
Fathers and Brothers of the Society of St. Paul,
2187 Victory Boulevard, Staten Island, New York 10314,
as part of their communications apostolate.

ISBN: 0-8189-0715-0

Printing Information:

Current Printing - first digit	1	2	3	4	5	6	7	8	9	10

Year of Current Printing - first year shown

1996	1997	1998	1999	2000

To the Memory of

The Reverend David J. Hassel, SJ
Author, Research Professor, Lecturer, Counselor

Biblical Abbreviations

OLD TESTAMENT

Genesis	Gn	Nehemiah	Ne	Baruch	Ba
Exodus	Ex	Tobit	Tb	Ezekiel	Ezk
Leviticus	Lv	Judith	Jdt	Daniel	Dn
Numbers	Nb	Esther	Est	Hosea	Ho
Deuteronomy	Dt	1 Maccabees	1 M	Joel	Jl
Joshua	Jos	2 Maccabees	2 M	Amos	Am
Judges	Jg	Job	Jb	Obadiah	Ob
Ruth	Rt	Psalms	Ps	Jonah	Jon
1 Samuel	1 S	Proverbs	Pr	Micah	Mi
2 Samuel	2 S	Ecclesiastes	Ec	Nahum	Na
1 Kings	1 K	Song of Songs	Sg	Habakkuk	Hab
2 Kings	2 K	Wisdom	Ws	Zephaniah	Zp
1 Chronicles	1 Ch	Sirach	Si	Haggai	Hg
2 Chronicles	2 Ch	Isaiah	Is	Malachi	Ml
Ezra	Ezr	Jeremiah	Jr	Zechariah	Zc
		Lamentations	Lm		

NEW TESTAMENT

Matthew	Mt	Ephesians	Eph	Hebrews	Heb
Mark	Mk	Philippians	Ph	James	Jm
Luke	Lk	Colossians	Col	1 Peter	1 P
John	Jn	1 Thessalonians	1 Th	2 Peter	2 P
Acts	Ac	2 Thessalonians	2 Th	1 John	1 Jn
Romans	Rm	1 Timothy	1 Tm	2 John	2 Jn
1 Corinthians	1 Cor	2 Timothy	2 Tm	3 John	3 Jn
2 Corinthians	2 Cor	Titus	Tt	Jude	Jude
Galatians	Gal	Philemon	Phm	Revelation	Rv

TABLE OF CONTENTS

Part III
WHERE THE PROPER MEANS
ARE FOUND TO ACQUIRE THIS PEACE

Part IV
ON THE PRACTICAL ASPECTS OF THIS PEACE

ACKNOWLEDGMENTS

This volume entitled: *A Treatise on Interior Peace* is the last of a series of books on St. Elizabeth Ann Seton initiated at the request of the late Pope Paul VI and his private secretary, Monsignor Don Pasquale Macchi, now Archbishop at Loreto, Italy, and were written with their special blessing. The typescript documentation for this work was made available by Monsignor Don Antonio Casieri, Director of the Postulators for the Causes of the Saints. Photocopies were procured through Monsignor Orazio Cocchetti of the Secretariat of State, Vatican City in June 1977.

The Reverend William W. Sheldon, C.M., Postulator-General for the Cause of St. Elizabeth Ann Seton, provided archival materials of the canonization process and ceremonies. Reverend Robert Bultman, Pastor at St. Francis Xavier Basilica and Custodian of the Brute Memorial Library at Vincennes, Indiana, made available the original French text of this book. A travel grant to Rome was obtained from the Medora H. Feehan Fund through the late John Cardinal Wright. For their kindness and solicitude, I am deeply grateful.

A special tribute of gratitude is due the late Reverend David J. Hassel, S.J., author, research professor, lecturer at Loyola University Chicago, to whom this book is dedicated, for his continued interest, valuable insights and untiring support of this work on St. Elizabeth Ann Seton, and for the Foreword and Epilogue to the *Intimate Friendships of Elizabeth Ann Bayley Seton*; to the Reverend George A. Maloney, S.J., famed Catholic theologian, author, and director of Contemplative Ministries, California, for the Foreword in this book; to the Reverend Anselm Romb, O.F.M. Conv., former editor of the Franciscan Marytown Press, for the publication of *Elizabeth Ann Seton: A Self-Portrait,* for the Foreword to *Elizabeth Ann Seton: A Woman of Prayer* and for reading the manuscript of *A Treatise on Interior Peace*; to the Reverend Robert T. Sears, S.J., professor of theology, Loyola University Chicago, for reading the manuscript of this book and for his valuable suggestions and insights.

My gratitude extends to Doctor Thomas J. Bennett, Associate Vice-President and Director of Research Services, Loyola University Chicago, for his continued interest and support in obtaining grants and for providing typing services; to Dr. Gerald W. McCulloh, Associate Director of Research Services, Loyola University Chicago, for his valuable assistance and encouragement; to Doctor Alice B. Hayes, former Academic Vice-President, Loyola University Chicago, for an honorarium; to Mary Donnelly and the Loyola Library staff; to the archivists at Saint Joseph's Provincial House, Emmitsburg, Maryland; at Mount St. Joseph's, Cincinnati, Ohio; at St. Elizabeth's Convent Station, New Jersey, at Halifax, Nova Scotia; and at the Ursuline monastery, Quebec, Canada. A special word of gratitude is due Sister Sara Louise Reilly, archivist at Seton Hill, Greensburg, Pennsylvania, and to Sister Rita King, archivist at Mount Saint Vincent's, New York City, for making available Elizabeth Ann Seton's handwritten translation of this book.

In addition, I am grateful to Monsignor Hugh J. Phillips, president emeritus, former archivist, and now chaplain at the National Shrine of Our Lady of Lourdes, Mount Saint Mary's College, Emmitsburg, Maryland, for his friendship and dedication to St. Elizabeth Ann Seton; to the Daughters of Charity for their warm hospitality; and to the Seton Hill Sisters of Charity for their unfailing support; to my family and friends, notably: Mother Richard Ann Watson, S.C., Sister Gertrude Foley, S.C., Sister Inez Mary Beckel, S.C., Dr. and Mrs. John W. Koenig, Mr. and Mrs. Robert White, Mr. and Mrs. Frank Cuzzolina, Dr. and Mrs. David Corso, Mr. and Mrs. John F. Cuzzolina, Jr., Mr. and Mrs. Lee

Pampel, Mr. and Mrs. Stephen Steinbeiser, Frank De Bernardis, Jeannette (De Bernardis) Paglia, Dr. Anie Sergis, Mr. and Mrs. Michael Spencer, Anthony Recchia, and Dr. and Mrs. Vincent Maturi.

Further, I wish to express my appreciation to the Reverends Eamon Carroll, O. Carm., Robert Trottier, M.S.C., Donald Brugger, S.J., Ralph H. Talkin, S.J., Carl Dehne, S.J., Angel Sierra, S.J., and Lawrence Reuter, S.J.; to the Reverends Monsignori Thomas E. Madden and Joseph M. O'Toole; to the Right Reverends William G. Connare and Norbert F. Gaughan, for their encouragement and interest in St. Elizabeth Ann Seton.

Lastly, my special thanks to Brother Aloysius Milella, S.S.P., Editorial Coordinator of Alba House Press and to Natalie F. Hector for typing this manuscript.

Sister Marie Celeste, S.C.
Seton Hill, Pennsylvania
Loyola University Chicago

Interior Peace

1st Chapter — It strengthens in us the love of God

All our piety should tend to our Union with God by knowing him and loving him — and establishing his reign in us by one absolute & continual dependance, a faithful correspondance with his interior communications & graces until he shall settle within us his kingdom of peace here; or call us to reign with him in his kingdom of glory. — — — — — — now without interior peace these dispositions can be but very imperfect in us... trouble interrupts and confuses our meditations, and the soul being weakened can no longer lift itself to god without difficulty, and the violent shocks she suffers is a continual disturbance to the solidity & tranquillity of his reign within her — and altho' he still has his throne in her heart it is a a tottering seat & threatens soon to fall, and being insecure cannot be the place of his rest. — as the prophet says (in 75 psalm) God dwells in peace — not but that he also has his habitation in the agitated soul of the just, but he is in it only as a stranger, because the confusion that reigns within does not permit him to converse familiarly with it, and its agitation & confusion threaten soon to banish his presence; drive him out ... a soul subject to violent agitations is seldom established in the solid ways of Justice — but when she has been a long while persevering in the way of peace she becomes like a house built upon a rock proof against winds & torrents — — — God makes his abode in it with delight & security, & this is the house he desires us to build for him (2 kings chap. 7) where he may reside perpetually & permanently, not choosing to dwell in those tents which are spread out at night to be removed in the morning, which move with every wind & have no firm solidity .. true emblems of a soul which agitated by its passions is in a state of continual uncertainty, always unequal, & contradictory with itself. — The saints have also suffered contradictions, and the waters of tribulation reached also to their hearts, their interior pains were also accompanied with troublesome temptations, but all these trials were as it were in the exterior only of the interior part always preserving its peace — — — God is not the interior of his Tabernacle — — —

FOREWORD

A universal *angst* or anxiety fills the heart of modern human beings with a sense of a loss of direction, of meaninglessness. Immersion in a pragmatic materialism has suffocated our communion with God deeply dwelling within our innermost self. We are adrift on a dark, stormy ocean that threatens our very meaningfulness.

Everyone the world over is continually discussing the important issue of peace. Yet how few of us human beings enjoy the peace Jesus promised to give His followers who would trust in Him as God's true peace: "Peace I bequeath to you, my own peace I give you, a peace the world cannot give, this is my gift to you" (Jn 14:27). We all eagerly desire true peace. Yet the plain truth in our hearts, in our families, neighborhoods, cities, countries, the world over is that there is no peace. With the prophet Jeremiah we can honestly say: "Peace! Peace! they say, but there is no peace" (Jr 6:14).

Dr. Viktor E. Frankl, the Austrian psychiatrist, confirms this almost universal sense of meaninglessness when we fail to live in the interior peace promised to us by Jesus Christ. He writes: "Effectively an ever-increasing number of our clients today suffer from a feeling of interior emptiness — which I have described as existential emptiness — a feeling of total absence of a meaning to existence." He attributes this existential emptiness to the loss of instinct in modern human beings and also the loss of tradition. "We no longer know what we must do by our instinct and we have lost the ability to know what we *ought* to do by cutting ourselves off from the roots of our past."

St. Elizabeth Ann Seton, the first American born saint and

founder of the Sisters of Charity, in her short span of forty-six years, worked indefatigably to establish Catholic schools through the religious Sisters of Charity which she founded in Baltimore, Maryland. She also wrote innumerable letters that reveal her deep piety and grasp of the traditional teachings found in Catholic writers that preceded her and rooted her and her nuns in the solid teaching of the Christian spirituality. She was fluent in speaking and writing in French and thus she has passed on to us a few of her translations of what she considered as traditional classics of Christian piety.

This present work on *Interior Peace* is basically her translation of what she considered to be a classic work on the subject of how a good Christian can develop the interior peace necessary to be open and receptive to hear and obey the Divine Word, Jesus Christ, living within each Christian. This work was written by the French Capuchin, Ambroise de Lombez, who published his work in Paris in 1756, twenty years before our American Revolution. This treatise became extremely popular in France through more than thirteen editions along with many translations into several European languages. Mother Seton's translation is the first American-English translation in the United States.

If a modern reader studies such a classic of Christian asceticism as this one on interior peace without some sort of understanding of the backdrop of the times in which the original French author lived and wrote, one would be all too quick to reject the work as irrelevant for our modern times. We can notice some evident influences from the neo-platonism of Augustinianism and something of the Jansenism found in the classic of *Imitation of Christ*.

But if the reader can separate the elements of a limiting cultural "baggage" from the kernels of deep and traditional truths taught by the universal, one and apostolic Church, then a great treasure would open up to that Christian. So many of the chapters here published from Ambroise de Lombez's classic on interior peace teem with deep insights that would be of great importance to any serious Christian eagerly striving to attain the most necessary interior peace promised by Christ.

The author highlights the importance of interior peace that helps us Christians of all times and of all cultures to dispose us in inner quietude and integration of body, soul and spirit levels to receive divine grace. The obstacles to such a peace that he outlines are equally applicable to all of us today: gloomy pessimism, vain striving for self-satisfying, illusory happiness, our natural business about many things with no priority to place God's Kingdom before all else. A very valuable and detailed treatment is given to the topic of scrupulosity which decimates all inner peace.

Today the same means are to be pursued by us moderns as those Christians in an earlier time such as humility, the ascetical practices that integrate us into a whole and receptive person open to God's communications, frequent communion, mental prayer accompanied by what Teilhard de Chardin called: *passionate indifference.* The author excellently outlines the inter-relationships between interior peace and the various inner temptations we daily have to resist, but such a struggle finds success only through interior peace that aids our openness to God in our weakness for only in His strength of His grace can we succeed to "bring into captivity and submission to Jesus Christ every thought and every imagination" (2 Cor 10:5).

The teaching of this book is consistent with that of all other earlier Christian spiritual authors from the great ascetics and mystics of the desert of the fourth century through the Middle Ages down to our present time. True contemplation of the indwelling Trinity is attained through purification which allows the contemplative Christian to be godly in the same love and humble service toward the indwelling Trinity and toward all other human beings. Inner peace can flow only out of inner love and joy which are attained in a continued process of moving through darkness and death to self-centeredness to enter into the light and life of the Christian vision where prayer is synonymous with purified love. This classic is grounded in the wisdom and prudence of St. Francis de Sales, yet is still solidly relevant to all modern Christians who seriously wish to attain that inner peace which comes from our union with the indwelling Trinity that is proved by the overflow of such peace into our zealous and loving service to our neighbor.

Reverend George A. Maloney, S.J.
Director — Contemplative Ministries
850 Coastline Drive
Seal Beach, California

March 19, 1995
Feast of Saint Joseph

PREFACE

Elizabeth Ann Seton, a saint for our times, was endowed with the *Ten Talents*, among them the gift of writing. A prolific writer, she is remembered for her letters to family and friends, her diaries and books of instruction, as well as her poetry and prayers. These works were obtained from the Congregation for the Causes of the Saints in Vatican City, Rome and served as documentation for three published books. Cf. Bibliography.

As an added dimension, fluent in the French language, Elizabeth translated numerous works from French to English which remain unpublished. They include the biographies of Saints and the works of notable French theologians. Cf. Bibliography. In this recent book: *A Treatise on Interior Peace*, Elizabeth demonstrates her language skills in translating a French classic into English. Written in Old French by the Reverend Ambroise de Lombez, a famed Capuchin theologian, it was first published in Paris in 1756.

From the outset, this book: *Traité de la Paix Interieure* gained enormous popularity and a reading audience sufficient to boast of more than thirteen editions in Paris. It was reprinted at Lyons, France in 1820, and at Lille, France in 1828 and 1836. More recently, it appeared again in Paris in 1922; and in 1961 the French-Canadian edition for Montreal, Quebec, Canada, was published by Fides in Paris.

In addition, it was translated into several European languages: A Catalan version appeared in 1771; the German version in 1840, and the Italian version in 1843. The first English version was published in Dublin, Ireland in 1840 and reprinted in Baltimore, Maryland in 1841. A later English translation was published by the Saint Anselm Society in London, England in 1892.

Approbation for the publication of this book was obtained from the Censor on February 19, 1756, signed *Boucher*; by order of the *Father General of the Order of Capuchin Minors*, it was read and signed on March 25, 1754 by two Capuchin theologians, F. Gabriel D'Auch, former Professor of Theology, and by F. D'Amasse de la Françoise, Professor of Theology. Permission for its publication was granted by the Reverend Father General of the Order of Capuchins on June 10, 1754 and was signed in Rome by F. Seraphinus (Capricollensis).

Further permission was given for publication by the Provincial Minister of the Capuchins of the Province of Aquitaine, France, signed April 1, 1756 at the Convent d'Auch by F. Clement D'Assain, Provincial, where Reverend Ambroise de Lombez was *Guardian*. The original text was dedicated to *Her Majesty*, the Queen (Marie Leszczynska, wife of King Louis XV).

How Elizabeth Ann Seton obtained a copy of the original French text is not exactly a mystery. In 1811, the Rev. Simon Bruté, an immigrant missionary from France, was appointed to Saint Joseph's Parish in Emmitsburg, Maryland, where two years prior to his arrival, Elizabeth Ann Seton had opened an academy for girls and was in the process of establishing a religious community of Sisters of Charity which she had founded. In a short time, Father Bruté became the spiritual director of Elizabeth's young community.

Whether Father Bruté brought a copy of the above mentioned book with him when he emigrated to America in 1811, or whether it was among the more than five thousand volumes that accompanied him to Emmitsburg, Maryland, on his return from a visit to his homeland in 1815, is not certain. Elizabeth Seton, however, frequently borrowed books from Father Bruté's personal library. These books are now preserved in *The Bruté Memorial Library* in Vincennes, Indiana.* It was there that the Editor of Elizabeth Seton's manuscript obtained what is believed to be the *only copy* of the original French text: *Traité de la Paix Interieure* in the

---

* The holdings of the Bruté Library now number 11,000 books.

Bruté Library holdings: Elizabeth Seton's translation follows carefully this text: the Ninth Edition, published in Paris, in 1769; it is said to be the copy Elizabeth Seton had utilized.

Elizabeth Seton's interest in French translation is manifold: a convert to Catholicism with great facility in speaking and writing the French language, and under the influence of the French clergy in Emmitsburg, Maryland, and in Baltimore, Maryland, Elizabeth was eager to enrich her religious background with Catholic thought and doctrine.

As a pioneer of Catholic education in the United States, and the founder of a religious community, she apparently found translating religious works instructive, stimulating, personally gratifying and necessary in fulfilling her task as a religious educator, at a time when religious works in English were not readily available.

Obviously, this book: *Traité de la Paix Intérieure,* which has survived the ravages of time for more than two hundred and fifty years, is a French classic. It involves an in-depth analysis of the psychological, philosophical and theological aspects of humanity. It is divided into four parts namely:

* The Excellence of Interior Peace;
* The Obstacles to this Peace and the Means to Conquer Them;
* Where the Proper Means are Found to Acquire this Peace;
* The Practical Aspects of Interior Peace.

Numerous chapter headings and other subdivisions are indicated in the Table of Contents.

To prepare this difficult work for the modern reader was nonetheless challenging. The present edition has undergone minor editorial changes in the format and presentation of the completed book in view of its publication. Emphasis was placed on clarity of expression; care was taken not to change or cloud the meaning of the original French text.

A *Treatise on Interior Peace* should attract and benefit the present day needs of a large and sophisticated reading public seeking peace of soul in today's troubled world, as well as educators, chiefly in the Human Sciences. It provides excellent reading for retreatants, both lay and religious. A new and revised edition, it is the first American-English translation of a great French classic published in the United States, and masterfully translated by Elizabeth Ann Bayley Seton, the first American-born saint, and a woman of Letters.

Sister Marie Celeste, S.C., Editor
Professor of Modern Languages
Loyola University Chicago
Seton Hill, Pennsylvania

March 25, 1995
Feast of the Annunciation of the Lord,
the day St. Elizabeth Ann Seton
received her First Communion, 1805.

INTRODUCTION

Elizabeth Ann Bayley Seton was born in New York City on August 28, 1774, two years before the outbreak of the American Revolution. She died in Emmitsburg, Maryland, on January 4, 1821, and was canonized at St. Peter's Basilica in Rome on September 14, 1975. She is universally acclaimed as the first native born American saint.

During her short life span of forty-six years, Elizabeth Ann Seton, a vibrant woman, is distinguished for her many accomplishments. In her early years, at the age of three, after the death of her mother (Catherine Charlton), Elizabeth as a loving daughter idolized her father, Dr. Richard Bayley, whom she claimed as her best friend. This friendship lasted beyond the grave.

At the age of nineteen years, Elizabeth Ann Bayley married William Magee Seton, a descendant of the royal family of Scotland of the Parbroath branch. A faithful wife, she became the caring mother of five children. At George Washington's birthday ball on February 22, 1797, for her social and charitable activities, she was acclaimed a society "belle."

On October 2, 1803, in search of a cure for her husband William's illness (incipient tuberculosis), Elizabeth, with Anna Maria, her eldest daughter, accompanied William to Leghorn, Italy, on the *Shepherdess* across the Atlantic ocean, to be the guests of the Filicchi family, long time friends and business partners of the Setons. Despite the warm welcome and kindness of the Filicchi brothers, Antonio and Filippo, and their wives, Amabilia and Mary Cowper, and despite Elizabeth's tender care and prayers during their quarantine in the Leghorn Lazaretto, William drew closer to God, but his health did not improve. He died at Pisa, fifteen miles from Leghorn, on December 27, 1803, and is buried in the English-American Protestant cemetery in Leghorn, Italy.

Eager to be with her children, whom she left in the care of her sister, Mary Post, and her sister-in-law, Rebecca Seton, Elizabeth and Annina, as she was then called, set sail on the *Pyomingo* accompanied by Antonio Filicchi for their return voyage to New York on April 8, 1804. After fifty-six days on the high seas, they arrived at the New York harbor on June 3, 1804.

Back in New York, Elizabeth's thoughts frequently reverted to William and her Filicchi friends in Leghorn. Fascinated by the Catholic practices in the Filicchi home and in the Churches she had visited in Florence and the surrounding area in Montenero, at Mass in the Shrine of Our Lady of Grace, Elizabeth was touched by faith in the real presence of Jesus in the Blessed Sacrament.

On March 14, 1805, Elizabeth made her act of abjuration at St. Peter's Church in New York City, and was converted to Catholicism. This action was taken contrary to the wishes of her Episcopalian pastor and close friend, the Reverend Henry Hobart, at Trinity Church in New York City. After much struggle and suffering, Elizabeth pinned her conversion on the Sacred Scriptures.

During the years 1804-1808, Elizabeth, now an impoverished widow and a single parent, struggled to earn a livelihood for herself and her children. Interested in their education, she made several attempts to ally herself with educators. For a time, she cared for ten boys as boarders at St. Mark's parish rectory. Later, she assisted Mr. William Harris, an Episcopalian clergyman and headmaster of a school in New York — a position she maintained despite the religious prejudice she had suffered. With the help of Antonio Filicchi, her sons William and Richard were sent to Georgetown College in Washington City, now Washington, D.C., for their education.

When Elizabeth was invited by the Rev. William Du Bourg, president of St. Mary's College in Baltimore, Maryland, to open a much-needed school for girls adjoining the College, she left New

York in early June 1808 on the *Grand Sachem*, a packet, with her three daughters, Anna Maria, Catherine Josephine and Rebecca, to pioneer Catholic education in the United States.

After being happily settled in her new home on Paca Street and seeing the new school growing in numbers, at the suggestion of the Reverend Pierre Babade, Elizabeth founded conjointly a religious community of women, the Sisters of Charity, to assist her in this work. By June 1809, upon the arrival of several candidates for the sisterhood, Bishop John Carroll of Baltimore bestowed on Elizabeth the title of Mother Seton, a title which has remained with her even today. On this occasion, Elizabeth Seton took privately her religious vows.

On June 24, 1809, Elizabeth with her daughters, her community and several students moved to Emmitsburg, Maryland, about fifty miles from Baltimore, Maryland in a covered wagon. With a happy heart, they trekked over the turnpike to take possession of the Fleming Farm, the gift of Samuel Sutherland Cooper, a seminarian and convert to Catholicism who wanted to further Elizabeth's work. Elizabeth called the thirty acre terrain, "St. Joseph's Valley," and the farmhouse was renamed the "Stone House."

When the farmhouse was not yet ready for occupancy, Elizabeth and her household resided at Mount St. Mary's retreat house across the road where they were warmly greeted by the Rev. John Du Bois, founder of Mount St. Mary's College for Boys. This happy situation lasted only several weeks.

On July 31, 1809, Elizabeth and her companions transferred to St. Joseph's Valley and the Stone House. From the beginning, it was obvious that a new and larger residence was needed for the Sisters and students. It was made from the logs on the farmland, and Elizabeth named it the "White House." The Sisters were officially known as the "Sisters of Charity of St. Joseph's (Valley)," and the school was christened "St. Joseph's Academy for Girls."

By early spring, students and Sisters were settled in their new Convent/School and St. Joseph's Academy was opened officially on May 10, 1810. Here Elizabeth Ann Seton had finally established her lifework, which lives on after her.

Today, the National Shrine-Basilica in honor of Saint Elizabeth Ann Seton is located in Saint Joseph's Valley, Emmitsburg, Maryland. Throughout the year, it is the site of numerous pilgrimages in her honor.

Part I

EXCELLENCE OF THIS PEACE

the milk of devotion like young children who know that it is good for them
but desire it also as reasonable children who know how to resign it, so
attachment to it will not a little retard our progress to the great work of
perfection & peace ... We may and we ought to enjoy the presence of our
Lord as long as he will remain with us .. follow him wherever he goes as
the Apostles did, follow him step by step every moment, run to him over
the very waves of the Sea like St Peter, rest ourselves on his bosom like St John
and yet if he withdraws, bear his absence without sadness or chagrin because
he certainly does it but for our good . " it is expedient I should go from you "
John 16. v. 6.

2.

If the absence of our Lord was necessary for the Apostles, and is still
necessary for Us, and if his visible presence could have been an obstacle
to the perfection of the Saints, what sensible good can there be even
spiritual, from which we ought not, to detach ourselves intirely ...
to wish absolutely to follow our Lord in his absence to endeavour to quit
the Earth & take a flight to heaven, is a reversion of his established
rules, & disturbing the order of his providence, and a useless unavai
fatigue -- Wait in peace till clothed with strength from on high .
wishing to be always at his right hand or his left is to know not what we ask
desiring to fix ourselves with him on Thabor is indiscreet and often proceeds
from a spiritual sensuality, or what is worse a secret vanity which
is still more despicable, more disagreeable to god, & injurious to ourselve
filling us with the desire of shining & being distinguished by favours & enthusiasms in piety, as
the body is adorned by the lustre of ornaments and graces. but wt
avails this subtile and deplorable ambition but to render Us bombaste
in devotion, as the vain and foolish are in their discourse & manner
and as insupportable to the eyes of God, as the vain & affected are in
the eyes of rational & sensible men . Conduct yourself before god
with great humility and simplicity , not with fervour and impatience
—— you desire to take your flight to heaven, to rise above the star

CHAPTER I

Interior peace reaffirms in us the reign of God.

All our piety should tend only to our union with God by knowing Him and loving Him; by establishing His reign in us through our absolute and continual dependence on Him; by a faithful correspondence to His interior communications and graces until He shall call us to reign with Him in His kingdom of Glory.

Without this interior peace, these dispositions can be but very imperfect in us: trouble interrupts and confuses our meditations, and the soul being weakened can no longer lift itself to God without difficulty; the violent shocks it suffers are a continual disturbance to the solidity and tranquility of His repose within it.

Although God still has His throne in our heart, it is a tottering seat and threatens soon to fall; being insecure it cannot be the place of His rest. As the Prophet [David] says in Psalm 75, God dwells in peace. That is not to say that He does not dwell in the agitated soul of the just, but that He is in it only as a stranger, because the confusion that reigns within does not permit Him to converse familiarly with it; its agitation and confusion threaten soon to drive Him out, to banish His presence.

A soul subject to violent agitation is seldom established in the valid ways of justice. But when a soul has been a long while persevering in the way of peace, it becomes like a house built upon a rock, against winds and torrents. God makes His abode in it with delight and security. This house, then, is the one that God desires us to build for Him (2 K:7) where He may reside perpetually and permanently. Not choosing to dwell in those tents which are spread out at night to be removed in the morning, and move with every wind, they have no firmness or solidity, are true symbols of the soul agitated by its passions in a state of continual uncertainty, always unequal and in contradiction with itself.

The Saints at times have also suffered contradictions, and the waters of tribulation, reached also to their hearts; their interior

3

pains were accompanied with troubled emotions, but all these trials were, as it were, only in the exterior of the soul; the interior part always preserving its peace. God is not moved in the interior of His tabernacle.

Chapter II

🦋 *It disposes us for the divine communications.*

This peace gives God an entire liberty to act within our souls, to enlighten them, to enforce them with His love, to lead them as He pleases. Whereas trouble creates a cloud which hides from us a part of its light, and a confused noise which prevents His voice from reaching us. Therefore, He says by His prophet (Ho 2:14-24) that He will lead us in solitude to speak to our heart. This solitude, so necessary to a sweet and familiar converse with God, consists in the silence of the soul, rather than in an exterior solitude which in itself is not capable of making us recollected.

The noise which arises in ourselves, and disturbs the powers of the mind on which God desires to act, distracts us much more than that which comes from without and strikes only the ear. One may be sensibly touched with the presence of God and be entirely recollected in the midst of a tumult of creatures as Ezekiel was amidst the confused sighs and groanings of a multitude of slaves (Ezk 1). But one can scarcely be recollected in the tumults of thought, in the emotions of passion and confusion of the soul. Besides God does not say He will lead us in solitude to speak to our ears but to our hearts. Therefore, He requires of us an interior solitude.

Without this silence of the soul, we should be solitary without being alone, and as St. Bernard says, a religious cell would be more an honorable prison than a holy retreat. To hear, like Mary Magdalene, the words of life which fall from the lips of Jesus, we must, like her, be in perfect repose and profound silence.

Thus, to have God within us and enjoy His communications, we must preserve ourselves in peace. Be *peaceable* and *humble* (says Kempis, Bk 2:8), *devout* and *tranquil*, and Jesus will remain with you. When leaving this world, He assured us He would remain with us to the end of ages, but He required of us to preserve His peace which He left with His apostles as a pledge of His love and an effect of His presence commanding them to carry it throughout the world with the light of His faith. "In whatever house you enter say: 'May peace be in this house'" (Lk 10), Himself giving the example, in the salutation, *"Peace be with you"* (Lk 24). St. Francis, made use of no other form of salutation (he says that God had revealed it to him). It is in truth an abridgement of every good wish; the church ends all her services by this wish of peace for this life, and of glory for the next; for after the glory of heaven, peace of soul is the best of all gifts.

CHAPTER III

It enables us to discover the movements of divine grace.

Another great advantage of this peace is that it enables us to discern the motion of God's grace within us from those of the evil one, or of our own self-love. The spirit of God produces peace and tranquility; the evil one on the contrary leads us always in trouble and dissipation. "I will hearken to the words which God will speak in my heart," says [David] the Royal Prophet, "for His words are the words of Peace" (Ps 84:9). The evil one may sometimes produce in us some appearance of this peace, and the complacency of *self-love* may make us feel something which approaches it. But an experienced soul will not mistake it, as one who has seen the light of the sun will not mistake the light of a lamp for midday. How essential it is in every detail of life to be able to discern the movements of God's spirit, from those which are not His! To how many mistakes are we subjected for want of this discernment of spirit and how much this peace (which next to faith, holy doctrine and obedience) is one of the most certain means to enable us to make it and ought to be valued by us.

How many scruples would be explained, and illusions dissipated; how many imprudences corrected and false devotions rectified if we never departed from this peace, which leads us to God without noise or trouble, or at least, if we would be guarded against whatever might disturb it within us! Though we should suspect whatever may disturb it, yet it may happen that a movement of divine Grace may be accompanied also with some emotion of our own; it is this latter which may disturb and trouble us. This is the general defect of persons of natural activity who introduce some degree of their own ardor in all their actions, and from the warmth of their imagination, cannot do anything in a peaceable manner for any length of time until by a long habit of peace and recollection, and perseverance, they succeed in moderating and subduing their natural activity.

Even for persons of this disposition, peace is a means of discerning the difference between that which proceeds from God or arises from their own natural temper. For, if at the moment they feel themselves animated with an ardent desire to perform the good they wish to effect, they would stop short at the moment, offer it to God, give themselves time to reflect, and quit their intention for awhile; they would soon find their ardor diminished, and their agitation subduing. If their design and intention proceeded from God, peace will remain alone in the bottom of their heart with that good will to which He has promised it; otherwise, this trial will make it all evaporate if the desire is only natural and human.

As long as this haste and interior fermentation continue, they should be persuaded that it is a proof of much natural activity and human motive in their conduct, and perhaps the only one on which it is founded.

Interior peace is then a mark by which we may know the movements of God within us. Not only does it enable us to discern them in their birth, but also in their effects. The more powerfully they operate the greater will be our peace. The labors even which we undertake by its influence do not trouble us, because they proceed from purity of principle which though infinite in its activity, is unalterable in its peace. It must, however, be acknowledged that we are apt to fall in some dissipation, even in a work of true and pure attraction, and it is seldom that this profound tranquility remains undisturbed, especially in our commerce with mankind.

The saints themselves have experienced it, the repose that Our Lord commanded His disciples to take when He drew them from the crowd after their return from their Apostolic mission (Mk 6) after labor as we were when we began it. The association with each other is apt to change in some degree that sweet association we enjoy alone with God — interior emotion is not considerable, and has no sensible effect while we are careful to limit our communications to what is only necessary.

The same divine movement which activates us always inspires this circumspection. It is at the same time a spur to excite us and a rein to control us; instead a false attraction excites us at once with eager desires, gives us no rest, leaves us no time for recollection, and far from inspiring us to circumspection, banishes even the thought of its being necessary in an action which aims only at what is good. Notwithstanding this desire which comes from the evil one or from our own will, however plausible its presence may be, it begins always with trouble and often ends by crime.

Chapter IV

It is a great defense against temptation.

What help does not this peace furnish us against temptations! In this state of recollection, of attention to our interior and of self-possession, nothing can pass within us without our immediately perceiving it. Thus temptations arrested in their very birth, and before they gain strength, are easily stopped in their progress.

In this interior silence, we hear on the first movement "the arrow that lightly flies by day, and the enemy that glides in darkness" (Ps 90): a thousand [arrows] fall at our left hand and ten thousand at our right, and not one shall reach us. Our salvation and strength are in repose and silence (Is 3:5). Our soul all recollected and, as it were, concentrated within itself, is so strong as to be in a manner impenetrable to its enemies, supported as it is also in other respects by the particular graces with which God recompenses fidelity.

Trouble, on the contrary, agitates in every way, disconcerts us and renders us as easy to vanquish as an army in disorder. Brothers are not distinguished from enemies where good order is broken, and worse still, poorly executed and where the number of combatants which ought to be its safety only increases its confusion. The great secret in danger is self-possession.

If our head should turn on the edge of a precipice, we must inevitably fall. At the sight of danger, terror seizes us, we tremble, the sight fails, the blood freezes, discernment and strength forsake us at the same time, and we are neither able to choose the means to withdraw us from danger, nor to make use of it: a true picture of a soul troubled by excessive fear in temptation. "Since my heart is troubled," says [David] the Royal Prophet, "my strength has failed, the light of my eyes is not with me, and I am buried in darkness" (Ps 37).

If, in this state, the soul is sustained, it can only be by a kind of miracle, and the help of singular grace, which God will not fail to give to those who do not render themselves unworthy by their infidelities. Would it not be an infidelity to yield to this inquietude which is always mixed with a secret want of confidence in God, as well as with our own weakness, to neglect the counsel of our Director who prescribes for us occasionally a firmer conduct, and finally to lose that peace which we so much wish to possess?

Besides these temptations from which we are preserved by interior peace, it also helps to defend us from those [temptations] which our own natural levity, and readiness to follow our own desires, very often occasion us.

<h2 style="text-align:center">CHAPTER V</h2>

It greatly helps us to know ourselves.

Another great advantage this peace procures us is a knowledge of ourselves, which cannot be acquired with a troubled interior. As in a quiet stream, we may distinguish the very smallest grains of sand, so when the soul is at peace, we can perceive our smallest imperfections; we see ourselves as we are, and consequently must feel that self-contempt which is an inseparable consequence of this knowledge.

From this contempt, humility arises which is the foundation of all the interior edifice. It is true that if we stop to contemplate with complacency this calmness and equality of mind, instead of considering the faults that disfigure it, it may create an interior pride in this case as well as in any other. For pride enters everywhere, since it lives even by its own destruction and is renewed from its own ashes. To avoid this damage, we must not fear, nor even perceive the advantage we possess in our peace, for as sheep do not quit their skins because wolves are sometimes clothed in them, said St. Augustine, so to abandon a good for fear of the vanity which may arise from the possession of it, is like becoming wicked for fear of being so.

If we consider ourselves in this state, only when purely necessary, with a simple and modest look as ones who, no longer vain of the advantages of nature, make use of a mirror to dress themselves with decency rather than for vanity, forgetting how they looked until they return again for the same purpose, as the Apostle James relates (1:28), thus contemplating some other person, as it were, instead of ourselves and the gift of God; not ourselves in the gift; seeing only His work in us, and with us; we

will not become self-complacent in our tranquility; we will perceive it proceeds not from ourselves, but on the contrary, that it is
incessantly disturbed by our own passions and levity, if the grace
of God does not restrain them.

Reflections of complacency will be banished by our simple
returns to God, and if they become more importunate, they must
only make us more vigilant to preserve our peace. They (these
reflections) cannot disturb, if they do not alarm us, but will even
increase our peace, if the temptation to vainglory brings us to
despise ourselves.

Chapter VI

It preserves us in simplicity.

Interior peace humbles us still more by the simple and modest
piety which it inspires in us. It affects no singularities, because all
that is not common and that it does not find in itself, is troublesome and contradictory to it. We neither see in it those sensible
fervors or those enthusiasms which carry the soul a great way
without bringing it much nearer to God; nor those animated
pictures which charm our imagination and give us a high opinion
of ourselves; nor the declining sweetness which, while it heats the
mind, weakens our constitution and still more our humility.

A new beginner is enchanted with these uncertain marks,
and makes every effort to obtain them, while the peace of the soul,
entirely neglected being less attractive and less flattering to our
vanity, is the more useful for our sanctification.

CHAPTER VII

It greatly assists recollection.

The necessity of recollection for an interior life is well known. All spiritual books speak of it in detail and prescribe different practices to attain it: good thoughts, attention to the presence of God, and others. For my part, I am persuaded that the means most necessary and subjected to the least inconvenience, and without which every other can be of little use is *Interior Peace*.

Other practices may apply us too much, sometimes amuse us, and often so far distract us as to interrupt the work of God within us. They do not commonly reach the source of our dissipations which is in our passions and activity; sometimes, they have no other effect than to heat the imagination. If they occupy the mind only, they are but a loss of time; if they go to the heart by the mind, it is a reversion. Can the application not be made directly to the seat of the good or the evil? It was to the heart of Jerusalem that God willed the prophet to speak (Is 40:2).

The shortest means to get rid of flying and useless thoughts, and to have none but such as are pious and good, is to cut off every motion of the passions, and be on our guard even against those which are holy and virtuous as soon as they disturb our tranquility. Let our heart be regulated, and all will be regulated within us. Let us be in peace, and our thoughts like the thoughts of God will be thoughts of peace (Jr 29:11). Those that trouble us have their source in the heart rather than the mind. The heart directs the mind as it wills and regulates it, but if led by passion it obscures the light of the mind.

The heart always has dominion within us; if it yields itself to humor, to caprice and impatience, it troubles and disconcerts all the interior and subjects it to itself; it is seldom that even the most reasonable mind can free itself from the slavery of a passionate heart. Is it to the slave or to the master that we must apply in treating for peace? While the former is not tranquil can the latter be recollected? If it were possible that it could be so, what kind of recollection would it be but an idleness and interior inactivity, or other stupidity in which the mind would not be properly free from distraction, but rather in a thoughtless state and secretly occupied with its own inaction until the heart, more tranquilized, shall furnish it with reflection or permit it to reflect in a connected manner.

Experience proves to us daily, that the most dangerous dissipation proceeds from the heart, and that a multitude of thoughts will not injure us materially, if they are not mixed with irregular affections, should the mind change from object to object either by necessity or levity; if the heart does not go out with it, our return to God will be easy, which is a sort of habitual recollection, less perfect, it is true, than the actual but which may be substituted for it!

If on the contrary, dissipation proceeds from the heart, or if it has entered in it, and above all, if it is established there, the evil will be great and the remedy difficult; all will be deranged. We will no longer find ourselves within, and nothing but a continuation of prayer, retreat, and mortification can restore us again to recollection.

Chapter VIII

Its many other advantages.

It would be endless to enumerate the advantages to be derived from this interior peace. It draws within our heart such inexpressible delight that sensible pleasure becomes insipid and distasteful after tasting its sweetness, which surpasses all we can conceive. By this sweetness, God draws us to His service and fortifies our hearts against sensuality. It forms in us an evenness of character and harmony of conduct which is most pleasing to God and delightful to all who behold it.

Without this peace, we are often from one moment to another so changeable and inconstant as to displease both God and man. It produces an air of modesty, sweetness, peace and simplicity, ingenuous and accommodating, which does honor to piety, and conciliates the esteem and affection of persons the most prejudiced against it.

In short, we may say of this peace what the Apostle [Paul] said of piety of which it is the soul and life, that it is good for all things, and obtains all kinds of blessings for us, both in the present life and for the future one (1 Tm 4:8).

If we wish to converse with God we must be in peace, for He speaks only the language of peace which can be easily understood only by those who are quietly recollected in their own heart (Ps 84:9). While we are in trouble, we speak a language different from His and cannot understand Him; if it may be so said, He does not understand us, and we become like strangers whom He knows not.

If we desire to be united to Him in holy communion, we must prepare a dwelling of peace for this King of Peace. It is in the retreat of the interior and the silence of the soul that we are to enjoy Him. The Paschal Lamb of the ancient sacrifice was eaten standing up and in haste: the loins girt and everything prepared for a journey. But the Lamb of the new sacrifice is eaten in the repose of the sanctuary in rest and peace.

Are we desirous of assisting our neighbor corporally? Do it in peace; without it, we are harsh, impatient, and disobliging even with the best intentions and most acceptable services. Would we serve them spiritually, our care must be still greater, for if the impatience of zeal should trouble the economy of your peace, we will speak without reflection and go further even than we intend. Instead of waiting for the moments of God, our own impatience alone will be heard, our grace and recollection will be lost, and the good we intended entirely frustrated, and more harm done to ourselves than we imagine.

In short, if we wish to work for our sanctification, remember

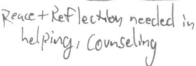
Peace + Reflection needed in helping, Counseling

it is the work of silence and of peace; or if we would labor for that
of others, we may be assured that to obtain an ascendancy over
their minds, and recommend the sacred precepts we wish to
inculcate, we must first recommend ourselves by our dispositions
of peace, and possess them so effectually as to shed their influence
on all who surround us.

This is an abridgement of the great benefits which result
from interior peace and which should make us estimate it as one
of the most signal favors of heaven; it is so precious a gift that God
does not impart it to the wicked, although He bestows on them
both talents and sanctifying graces (Is 48). It has always been so
well understood to be a particular gift of His bounty and a mark
of His divine presence that the false Prophets spoke of nothing but
peace to persuade their hearers that they spoke to them from God;
but there could be no truth where God was not, for He is the God
of peace in the midst of His saints as a father in the midst of his
family.

Those who preserve with most care the peace of their heart
are the most cherished of His children. "Blessed are the peacemak-
ers (the peaceable), they shall be called the children of God." He
loves them with tenderness; He bears them in His arms; they
repose tranquilly in His bosom. I will sweetly rest in peace with
God, says the Prophet [David], and my rest in Him shall be as a
delightful sleep (Ps 4).

If the acquisition of this interior peace is difficult, our wish to
possess it should be but the more ardent, as this difficulty is a new
proof of its excellence. What is easily obtained is not commonly of
great value. It is not surprising that both nature, and the *Enemy* to
which it is in contradiction should trouble it. These means will
now be detailed.

Part II

TREATMENT ON THE OBSTACLES TO THIS PEACE AND THE MEANS TO VANQUISH THEM

but little. Commune often, and many times a week if it is by the advice of a pious enlightened and prudent director. If your Attraction to this adorable Sacrament is accompanied with a sense of your unworthiness and you join to it the practice of goodworks, flight from the World, a life of recollection and Mortification long tried, seperation from all sin even venial, I say seperation not exemption, which is incompatible with human frailty, a sincere desire of advancing in virtue, watchfulness over yourself as far as your Situation permits -- Commune I say altho' you appear to present Nothing to Jesus but a dry heart and a mind envelopped in darkness. Remember darkness praises God as well as light, and we may present ourselves with confidence in his Sanctuary in this state of aridity on which He delights to display the lustre of his Glory.

Chapter 3.

Chapter 3ᵈ { we are not to be troubled by our
distastes and fickelness —

After all that has been said on aridities and distaste, when we were considering the means of acquiring peace; it remains now to apply our observations. - And however little taste we may have for holy exercises yet persevere in them constantly and preserve your peace equality of conduct. should your prayers become an insipid, and even a troublesome employment, bear it patiently, and join to the sacrifice of the lips, that of the privation of sensible enjoyments. carefully banish from your mind that too common error of imagining that the Almighty no longer accepts the sacrifice of praise when it proceeds from our heart is shut-up, since on the contrary it is when it is most afflicted he most desires the offering of it, by which we draw down his grace, light, and joy. be strengthened then by the persuasion that the greater your difficulty is in praying, the more agreeable your prayer = is to God, and

Chapter I

Of vain joy and gloomy sorrow

Excess of joy is one of those causes which most commonly derange us within. We are not guarded against it because it presents only pleasure, and that pleasure often innocent; we feel not the wounds it gives us because the very first we receive is from inattention which makes us insensible to those which follow, and even unconscious of our danger. Inconsiderate and dissipating, it creates in us a sort of rarefaction or giddiness which expands our minds on every object, as water thawing, or melting wax and leaves nothing in the vessel it runs out of, but dried dregs at the bottom (Ps 21); an enemy to reserve and mortification, it even tempts us to forget the bounds of modesty.

This excess of joy and foolishness opens the door to all the senses, admits every exterior object which present themselves, and uniting with the senses, they put all within us in motion, and excite a tumult which does not permit us to enjoy a moment of repose. Tumultuous joy producing loud laughter, high speaking, delivering us up to every inconsiderate sally of the imagination, though not indulged to the last extreme, yet the harm it does us is always considerable: a quarter of an hour of trifling folly will dissipate the fruit of many days of recollection; all interior grace must disappear in such commotion from whence a thick vapor arises which obscures the soul and tarnishes its luster. Much time and compunction are required to regain the fervor and peace which dissipation deprives us of.

Sadness affects us in a manner quite different, but it equally deprives us of peace. Joy dissipates us, and sorrow absorbs us; peace is in the middle, but very distant from both. It would be in vain to attempt describing all the ill effects of a gloomy and chagrined humor; everyone knows that it is the certain destroyer of interior calm, and when it extends externally, renders us touchy, timid, impatient, and insupportable to others and to ourselves. In this state, we seem to have lost all the talents of nature and of grace; they are, as it were, all buried under the ruins of the interior edifice. We can scarcely form a good thought; nothing is present to the mind but objects of affliction and sometimes even of obscenity. We fly from man, without approaching to God; we obtain neither the merit of recollection, nor the ease of dissipation.

There is a sorrow which is of God, as also a joy we taste in Him. The Apostle [Paul] exhorts us to enjoy always the latter, and he was happy that the Corinthians felt the former. This was the joy of Mary in the arms of St. Elizabeth, and her sorrow at the foot of the cross. Both contribute to the peace of the soul instead of troubling it; the one acts upon it as a bridle to our levity; the other as a comfort to our weakness. There is nothing of evil in either, but in their excess. This excess begins only when the interior is troubled. It is then that the words of the wise men are applicable, "This joy is folly" (Si 7:5), and that sorrow is the source of many evils (Si 25:17).

We must repress all excess of joy and sorrow in their very inception; for if we suffer either to gain ascendance, it will be difficult to recover our peace of soul. They are two opposites which mutually destroy each other; yet they may be usefully employed in suppressing the excess of either, by exciting ourselves to holy joy when we feel inclined to sadness, and when joy would prevail using the restraint of Salutary Sadness to repress its excess. Both extremes must be avoided; a tranquil and modest joy is the just medium. If the fear of falling into either of these defects should excite its contrary in us, to avoid the danger, we must pass between them both. We bend the body on the opposite side to that which we fear to fall, not that we wish to fall on that side rather than on the other, but to prevent falling at all. Thus, we should endeavor to preserve its balance between these two passions until it gains a settled equality of mind.

CHAPTER II

Impetuous zeal

Too lively a zeal will also trouble this peace. All who are animated with this zeal will do everything with force and with heat, and seem to make it a point of conscience to avoid that moderation so necessary to the tranquility of the soul. It is quick to take whatever is good or appears to be good — ardent in its execution, and impatient to finish it. That prudence which stops to reflect before it determines is considered either negligent or too political; a moderation which acts with reserve is taken for indolence and inactivity; modesty which waits with patience, and without any sensible expressions of pleasure, the event of its pious intentions is called indifference to good.

If it withdraws in Solitude, it becomes like an owl seldom to be seen, abhorring the light, a true misanthrope which we should avoid encountering as we never can meet it with impunity. If it takes a fancy to come forward in order to do some good, it flies here and there in continual action not allowing itself a moment of rest. Should it resolve on mortification? It knows no bounds and in a short time the health is destroyed; and when it is necessary to restore it, indulgence is carried to an equal excess. Is it in question to quit a dissipating or too natural attachment, instead of patiently and insensibly dropping it? All is in extreme without any consideration and opposed to all discretion.

The faults of others awaken the ardor of this zeal, which is always ready to take fire; a child of thunder wishing to extirpate all the Samaritans. Indiscreet and imprudent zeal without respect for superiors or consideration for equals, or condescension for inferiors, it requires perfection from everyone; nor does it perceive that its own impatient desire is in itself a great imperfection. Not that it is neglectful of itself or pharisaical in its dispositions, it exacts yet more from itself than from others; hastening and pressing forward in the path of virtue, it exhausts both body and mind. Its faults torment and tempt it to despair.

Sad, confused, dejected and distressed, it has no courage to resume the path it has strayed from, and is on the point of abandoning all. Never can we possess true peace while we are the sport of the sallies, caprices and vexations produced by this zeal as a feather agitated by the wind. Eagerness is perhaps the most frequent trouble of the interior peace of devout souls, at least it is that which most frequently contradicts them.

Occasions of passion and dissipation but seldom occur in a life of retirement, but objects or occasions of zeal are never wanting. Oh! How many pretexts will our natural restlessness allege to justify its ardor! God is offended; those who commit the evil will be lost; they who witness it will be scandalized. The error must be discovered in the beginning and stopped. Thus spoke the hasty and imprudent laborer of the Gospel: "Shall we go and tear up the vile cockle?" But the father of the family more prudent and tranquil, though not less zealous, forbids them, and restrains their activity, giving them time to cool from the time of seed sowing until harvest.

The spirit of impatience knows not what it does; in its first access, it can make no discernment, all is confounded; in its precipitation, it treads the good grain under foot in running after the bad; both are pulled out together because they are mixed indiscriminately.

Why not (in this eagerness to do good) why not stop first where the evil is most pressing and closest at hand? Why not turn our ardor upon our own necessities, and insure to ourselves the first fruits of our zeal which would prepare us for improvement. Otherwise, it is to be feared that our labor will all be lost, and we will only increase the evil we would repress, by the impatience which blinds us.

To moderate this impatience, we should leisurely consider the difficulties it brings us by the hastiness, trouble and scandal it involves us in. By repressing its sallies, and endeavoring even to banish the reflections it suggests to us, waiting, if possible, until we obtain the moderation in our desires that characterizes the zeal which comes from God before we resolve to follow its dictates.

Zeal leads to impatience?

CHAPTER III

Natural Activity

That natural ardor which easily excites impatience and vivacity has nearly the same marks as impetuous zeal, and is as much in contradiction with interior peace. It is also certainly a source of this zeal which would not be impatient in itself, if our temper was not so. Follow these ardent Zealots in their ordinary actions, and it will be found they are the same in these as in their works of piety. Everything is hurried and confusion; nothing is accomplished with the speed they desire. Adopting a high and decisive tone of voice, they neither can praise or blame with moderation. Everything is excellent or detestable; every action and word is accompanied by quick motions and animated looks. They cannot walk, but must go in haste, and this temper, like a devouring fire, dries up and consumes the body as well as the soul. Always in motion, always changing, and uncertain in its appearance, it is a mercury without consistence, as restless as that which is drawn from the mines. Never can we obtain repose until by correcting this excessive activity, we obtain the possession of ourselves.

Not that we should awaken from its ashes the apathy of the ancient philosophers or annihilate the powers of the Soul, with the false contemplatives of the lost Ages. Let us act, and act in earnest as long as we are able to act thus. But let us act with mildness. This is in the power of everyone. It is our own fault when we lose the advantage of possessing it. Let us be active, if we are so by nature, but instead of allowing our vivacity to run away with us, we should always keep it restrained and limit it to the bounds of just moderation.

To succeed in this, we should avoid whatever may excite us to passion. I do not mean those gross and criminal passions which tear the heart; those who are possessed by them would not aspire to this peace or even know what it means. It would be as ridiculous to speak to them of interior peace, silence and repose in God, as to exhort a Parricide to tranquility and sleep while he is enclosed in a sack with a wolf and an asp in punishment of his crime, but I speak of certain delicate passions which disturb and shock it, and destroy that equanimity it should enjoy to preserve its self-possession and union with God.

Interior calm is so delicate that it may be altered by the smallest cause just as the slightest wind may ruffle the surface of a smooth water. This caused St. Bernard to grieve and complain that notwithstanding the deep recollection and austerity of his interior mortification, yet nothing continued quiet within him, and he experienced an agitation in every power of his soul because this subtlety of his passions penetrated to all of them. Even innocent pleasure, sacred friendships, useful knowledge, and certain desires permitted to everyone may produce this effect.

The calm of our soul is disturbed by the excesses of our nature, and these must be repressed. It is easy to find the means, but not so easy to practice it with any perceptible success which is only obtained by perseverance. The more difficult the success, the greater will be the recompense, and consequently, the greater should be our zeal. The application of our vigilance brings encouragement in our weakness, and consolation in our pains. St. Francis de Sales combatted this activity of temper for many years and succeeded perfectly; should we not think the labor too much, or despair of success? A warm and animated temper, like a fiery courser, may carry us a great way, but in order that it may neither throw us nor fatigue us, we must hold its reins short.

We should treat ourselves as we treat an unruly child whom we wish to be more discreet as soon as it begins to raise its voice, or show any signs of passions; we cast on it a look of severity to recall it to recollection. It is from our imagination that this warmth generally arises, yet not always, nor even from the emotions of the heart, but sometimes from the temperament of our body, in which case the aid of medicine may be a necessary assistance to virtue.

CHAPTER IV

Indolence

In order to restrain activity, we must not yield ourselves to indolence, or the remedy will be worse than the evil. Of all the defects we have named, indolence is most opposed to interior peace which is only granted to courageous souls, and is the recompense and fruit of their fervor. Our idea of it would be very false, if we imagined it to consist in a stupid and immovable indifference because it is calm and quiet, or that its tranquility arises from an aversion to activity rather than self-possession which would be making its habitual gentleness an habitual laziness. This peace, on the contrary, is an equilibrium acquired by persevering care, a *repose of the soul* in God not in the tomb of the body; a regular movement of the passions corrected and harmonized, not a deep and senseless lethargy which nothing can pique or awaken; a delicious food drawn from the mouth of a vanquished lion, not a shameful slumber of self-indulgence. This manna hidden in the heart is the prize of our victory, the fruit of courage and laborious patience.

When we feel within us a disposition of indolence, we should incessantly endeavor to shake it off as we would try to get rid of a lethargy; to reanimate ourselves by activity and manual labor, as we would shake our limbs when the blood stagnates. Great masters of the spiritual life counsel in this case corporal austerities which like a sharp instrument rouses stupefaction; but great moderation is necessary in this remedy.

indolence = inclination towards laziness

CHAPTER V

On the violence of temptations and its resistance

The violent efforts we make against temptations are a great
hindrance to the peace of soul. Agitated and tormented in this
state by the enemy, and often still more by our own impatience, all
is trouble and commotion. The mind becomes excessively affected, the blood violently agitated, the pulse convulsive, the
breathing quick and short: the imagination is inflamed, the head
heated, and the breast exhausted. Tranquility and silence might as
well be looked for in a breach where an assault is made and
received with equal rapidity. This is certainly not the right way to
resist temptation, but often the means of augmenting the danger,
and always of creating more trouble.

     Not that we should remain totally inactive when we are
tempted; this would be a worse extreme than the other, infinitely
more damaging. The best rule would be to guard against both by
a medium strong and resolute, but firm and tranquil. Without it,
we may be easily disconcerted, and before our composure is
regained, the enemy may have time to gain an advantage and
deprive us of our peace of heart and soul, recollection and devotion. Patience, vigilance, prayer, confidence in God, diffidence of
ourselves, avoiding the occasions of sin, disavowing the impressions of temptations when they arise and forgetfulness of them
when they disappear, these should then become our only resources.

Chapter VI

Some other obstacles to this peace

There are also many other things which trouble interior peace which I will mention but slightly, such as the intrigues and dissimulations of the mind which keep us in constraint, always on thorns, unequal and inconsistent, appearing to be what we are not; human friendships which bind us, dissipate the mind and subject us to an excessive attention which is contrary to interior attraction and often to conscience itself; that little self-love (for violent passion is not here in question) that attachment to the senses, to conveniences, to reputation, to self-will which fills the mind with teasing thoughts, impatient desires, sorrowful reflections and foolish delicacies; the secret vanity of being possessed of knowledge, wit or birth or, perhaps, even of devotion itself, and the ideas we have formed of it, the reputation of it we have acquired and, in short, of all our talents both in nature and in grace. Vanity which raises or defects us, in proportion to the praise or blame we receive often interrupts our recollection, subjects us to every caprice of others or our own (as a kite which is driven by every wind) to dissipation which draws us out of ourselves; imagination which seduces or distracts us, long conversations which dissipate the mind; attachments which weaken the heart and are always incompatible with liberty of soul (whatever may be the quality of the creature which excites them); in general, to whatever awakens passion and draws us from that repose which can be enjoyed only in God.

The irregularities of the mind always disturb the serenity of the soul, that serenity which purifies its thoughts, adds a merit to its actions, oftentimes consoles us, and dissipates our scruples; serenity which after the Law of God and the particular duties of every state, decides almost the whole of our conduct and even, as it were, our eternal salvation. The innate peace it procures to us is the foundation and materials for every good work, and of all

virtues. It is that daily and habitual peace which honors God,
disposes us to contemplation, and leads us to the divine union. It
is that divine balm which gives on earth a foretaste of that which
is enjoyed in heaven, and that we should endeavor to procure by
every possible means.

*So that we may possess it without interruption, we must be simple
and ingenuous without being imprudent; speak of all things in a noble
and elevated manner, yet without haughtiness; avoid human friendships, without incivility; see all things, and bear all things without
looking at anything, or hearing anything more than necessity requires;
preserving always a gravity and seriousness worthy of that God whom
we serve, and the blessed eternity we aspire to.*

*We should avoid amusement as a weakness of infancy; cut short all
useless conversations, and suffer nothing unnecessary to enter in those
which are useful. We must also moderate our pleasures and pains, using
pleasures with reserve when obliged to yield to them, and receive pains
with tranquil submission, if unable to support them with joy.*

CHAPTER VII

Of scruples

1.

Nothing more frequently disturbs peace in a timid soul than
scrupulosity which devours it. This destroying evil no more
permits the soul to be tranquil than a tyrannic master [does] the
slave whom he governs. His slightest faults are judged to be
crimes; his best actions are badly done; his duties never sufficiently accomplished, and when a hundred efforts are made to
amend them, the enemy of repose is equally dissatisfied. Like a
tiger, it pursues his timid, trembling prey and disquiets the soul
even in sleep by terrifying dreams; in prayer by indecent images,
the very fear of which is sufficient to produce them; in Commun-

[handwritten note: Scrupulosity = Obsessive desire over ones sins and compulsive performance of religous devotion.]

ion by aridities inseparable from violent combats which it makes use of as a proof of the bad state of conscience; in confession, yes, even in his confession (where the greatest sinners find a source of sweet consolation) this innocent soul suffers a cruel torment. Hesitating and uncertain from fear of diminishing his faults or magnifying them, of deceiving the confessor, or himself, of failing to mention some circumstantial minutiae that the scruple magnifies before his eyes, trembling he accuses himself. The absolution that he will receive serves only to increase the pain.

Thus, this cruel enemy of souls turns even the duties of piety to its own account — these same duties which ought to be the best means of overcoming scrupulosity. The greatest desire of performing them well, however great the desire may be, is no security against the tormentor who converts it to his own advantage. This wish of exactness which the innocent soul so much desires as a consolation turns into an excessive apprehension of failing in a pious exercise, and then represents these very fears, not as proceeding from zeal to do well, but as the effect of abominable negligences and indifference in the service of God.

Where then are the resources of a soul so beset? Will this unfortunate soul seek distraction in the company of the virtuous, or look for consolation in his own sufferings? Intruding objects, freedom of conversation, careless thoughts passed over in moments of distraction without being checked with its customary care, or detested as usual with all its might; all these unite and combine to convert to poison the most innocent and lawful pleasures of society, so needful to re-create it and so necessary to its situation.

Shall the soul retire to the shelter of solitude? Ah! it is there that the enemy awaits him to exercise its utmost power; alone and unoccupied, without counsel or support, he regains with advantage that influence which a few moments of reprieve had deprived him of; accusations now become capital; proofs quite clear, and condemnation certain. Shall the fearful soul cast itself in the arms of divine mercy, the secure refuge of the wretched? It is no resource for this soul; the cruel enemy deprives the soul of it by a lively painting of his imaginary crimes against God, and of God's anger against it, still more imaginary; that tender and paternal bosom in which she (the soul) sometimes throws herself in a despairing kind of transport, rather than by a tender attraction of love and confidence. That divine and paternal bosom from which she imagines herself to be repulsed with indignation becomes for her a place of terror and dread.

In the end, sorrowful, weighed down and disconsolate, she abandons herself to tears. Who in such excess of affliction can restrain them? Who can have a heart insensible to this grief? But her tears will not remedy the evil; on the contrary, the evil besets her and grows stronger by her weakness. Can peace be found in so miserable a state? It may as well be looked for in the torments of cruel torture as on a rack.

2.

The scrupulous soul is, indeed, an object of compassion. It fears God; but that fear is its torment. It loves Him, but that love is without consolation. It serves Him, but serves like a slave; it is galled and oppressed by that yoke which is sweet and easy to the rest of His children. It generally has the best dispositions for interior peace: solitude, recollection, mortification. But scrupulosity renders all these virtues useless, and often even destroys them.

In short, those in this state of scrupulosity may be envied for their virtues, while their sufferings claim all our compassion, since in this life they endure the torments of the next (at least comparatively). In proportion to the extent of the scruples is the difficulty of their cure; for where shall the remedy be found when neither their own reflections, nor the sufferings they endure, nor the experience of how often they are imaginary, nor the conviction of the illusions of their imagination which have been manifested to them again and again, nor the patience and authority of their confessors have been able to affect it.

The more deplorable their state is, however, the greater should be their endeavors since if they are left to themselves, the evil augments continually and the consequences must be fatal. The loss of interior peace is not the least; but great as is that loss, it is not always the greatest. Alas! to what disorder will not gloomy and ungovernable passions lead in a temper naturally ardent and impetuous, and to whom the service of God has become a torment and slavery?

There are examples of scrupulous persons who, from an excess scrupulosity to excite compassion, have passed to a state of libertinism the most abandoned. Besides, their piety merits our special care, and if they would add to it docility, the best fruits would be reaped from it. But this subject must be referred to the many learned writers who have treated of it, as the plan of our observation must be restricted to short maxims.

3.

Scruple arises either from an inability to discern between mortal and venial sin; between the thought and the reflection; between the inclination and the will; negligence and conceit; or between melancholy affliction which fills the mind with sorrowful thoughts and renders the heart accessible to whatever may afflict it, or a heated head which gives a powerful tension to the fibers of the brain rendering them sensible to every different motion as the chords of an instrument highly strung, from whence arises a confusion of thought which cannot be unraveled, neither from natural timidity which is easily alarmed, nor from a vivacity of imagination which paints in lively colors whatever we fear, and renders these objects so present to the soul that it knows not how to escape them, or in an excessive desire of certitude in whatever relates to salvation; or from the merciful conduct of God who by these pains of the mind (infinitely more afflicting than those of the body) purifies the soul; from the malice of the enemy, who distresses the innocent soul he cannot corrupt; or finally from secret pride which desiring to excel in all things, becomes confident and abandons itself to its own guidance.

In the first case, the instructions of an enlightened director are necessary; in the second, the help of a good physician; in the third, rest, sleep, proper recreation, a sufficiency of good nourishment, and pure air. In the fourth case, we must rouse and animate ourselves with courage and resolution, seldom indulge in sorrowful or dejecting reflections, even of our own corruption, the empire of our passions, the difficulties of salvation, the depths of God's judgments, the severity of His justice. But often reflect on whatever may excite our confidence and fill the heart with firm and generous courage, such as the view of the power of divine grace to vanquish our most terrible enemies, the infinite goodness of God, His love for us, His eternal and ardent desire for our salvation, all He has done to promote it giving us even His own and well beloved Son, delivering Him up to the most cruel and shameful death — the divine greatness and the high destination of our souls formed in the image of God, continually protected by His angels and inheritors of His glory.

This advice is not suited to those who are scrupulous from timidity, for it we except those who are so from presumption and by divine permission in order to humble their pride, it is useful to all. Even those who are not timid by nature become so as soon as they yield to *scruple*. It is a malady which renders them susceptible to the most sorrowful perplexities. If the vice is in the temperament, it can scarcely be cured. Impressions arising from natural disposition are obstinate and difficult to remove, but patience and resolution may at last be victorious.

4.

If the evil comes from the *imagination*, those phantoms it presents must be carefully banished, and it must never be made use of but through actual necessity and with much precaution as a knife with two edges which may cut with one side while we use the other, and especially turn a deaf ear to it when the question is of faith, or its own pains or doubts. It is a passionate, seducing, decisive advocate which makes the judge lean to whichever side it pleases, or at least will so dazzle by its own eloquence as to prevent the possibility of a just discernment. Free yourself then of all prepossessions, consult only reason, adhering to it alone. Hearken to the counsel for and against; you will find it wise, just, and disinterested, uniform and exact, and the judgment will be as sure as the counsel is prudent.

5.

A scrupulous person may judge correctly enough of themselves on the first view of their case, but if in order to tranquilize a threatening trouble they examine it with too much care, the imagination becomes heated in spite of themselves, their reason clouded, and what first was certain, now becomes doubtful, and often from a habit of self-condemnation, their judgment becomes fixed and decided. Scrupulous persons should judge of themselves as we look at colors of a strong hue, by slightly glancing the eye over them. If we gaze on them too long, they hurt the sight.

6.

We may endeavor with certain limitations to find out if, indeed, we are in the way of salvation; but this enquiry should be regulated with great prudence. A wish to pass the bounds it prescribes would be an intemperate and fruitless effort. There must always remain in us an obscurity to humble us, but it ought neither weaken our courage nor tempt our curiosity. To seek an evidence of our soul's salvation is only tempting God, and trying to discover what He has determined to conceal, and cannot make known to us but by a supernatural light, known only to some of the greatest saints and even to them, rarely and by quick and fleeting light, and which it is even best we should be unacquainted with.

7.

God Himself assures you that you may walk without fear under the guidance of those He has charged with your direction, that when you hear them, it is Himself you hear, and He considers the obedience you show to them as shown to Himself, or on the contrary when you show them contempt, it is Himself you despise; that He has given them command to watch over you, and you may depend upon them as upon guardians and sentinels who are charged to answer for your soul, and even for your mistakes, if they proceed from their advice and not from your indocility.

After all these assurances, you still require certainty before you will go a step. This is either a want of faith or presumption — want of faith, if you believe not the word of God; presumption, if you refuse subjection to the order established. To wait for the daylight before you proceed is either to want confidence in your guide, or to refuse his assistance.

8.

No, you will reply, it is not my wish to guide myself. I will obey the guide appointed for my soul, and my obedience would be entire, if his conduct was more perfect. Some trifles displease you in his manners, and your fear of being misled aggravates you extremely. Suppose this is so and even worse. He may not be a fervent priest, but he is a good confessor. Perhaps he possesses not that recollected piety full of tenderness and grace that you desire to find in him, but he tries to lead you to it. Should he be unworthy of these gifts, he would be not less the channel of them for you. The grace of his vocation will not be taken away for his personal defects. The best physicians do not always enjoy the best health, nor is their regimen always most exact. Choose your confessor with care and discernment, and then go simply and confidently as he directs.

9.

Be yet more indifferent with respect to his talents than his manners. Make choice of talents when it is in your power; seek them even and attach yourself to them when you meet them united with probity and prudence. But if you do not find them, or find them alone, do without them and remember, that it is not talents but the promises of God and the Authority of the ministry which are your security. Take what you find best suited to your ability and obey blindly. God will accomplish His work in each one of us by His own means. Whether He nourishes you as He did His Prophet Elias [Elijah] by the ministry of birds or of angels, you ought to be equally satisfied because in Him alone your whole confidence should be placed.

10.

Scrupulous persons imagine their love for God is great, while yet they have many hesitations in His service which seem more the product of self-love. So much delicacy in their way of thinking, and measured exactness of manner, are very striking characteristics of vanity and often proceed from no other source. They desire to be, and yet more to see themselves always exact and in regular order. Their faults of negligence give them vexation, and this vexation throws them in trouble — trouble produces scruples. You cannot pardon yourself a fault, you will say. Begin then by attacking your too good opinion of self, which if you spare it, will turn against you, and will prove to be the most cruel of tyrants.

11.

Thus, I believe, scrupulosity takes its origin in many forms. In the beginning the scrupulous are much occupied with themselves, continually making representations to their director, and entertain doubts in order to discuss them. A habit is formed insensibly; the mind is more and more engaged in examinations which at every moment occur on the minutest actions, and most trifling doubts. These doubts become inevitable and cruel perplexities at last, and from having at first reflected on self with too much complacency, they are soon under the painful necessity of reflecting on them with chagrin.

12.

Doubts are the torments of the scrupulous; to restore peace to their souls they should banish them. For those who are not under the influence of this malady a doubt is a doubt; for those who are, a doubt is almost a certainty; for of what do they not doubt in their continual perplexities; they doubt even of their doubts, if they reflect too much upon them. Nothing can be more confused than their ideas, or more embarrassing than their conversations on their imaginary pains. Though of those which are real, none can be more precise, correct, and decisive than theirs. Error produces only troubles and confusion; truth only certainty and conviction. When scrupulous persons declare without hesitation that they have failed in a point of duty, they should surely be believed, but not until then.

13.

To endeavor to silence scruples by reasoning is the same as rubbing an earthen vessel until it becomes transparent. We must cut short the imagination, and treat it as an idiot who can never be silenced but by leaving it to its own folly. But a scrupulous soul resolves to listen to its scruples once, and only once, and then to silence them, like a hydropic who will take but a glass of water to satisfy one moment. It augments its thirst, increases his malady, and excites its desire to drink without ceasing.

14.

Like a hypochondriac, so is it with a scrupulous person. He is at the same time sick in reality, and sick in imagination. He reflects continually; he consults, takes an infinity of remedies for complaints he has not, and thinks but little of remedying those which he has, and even thinks those are blind who speak to him of them. Obedience to a skillful physician, attention to friendly advice, and if it may be so said, a forgetfulness of self are the means of cure both for the one and the other.

15.

Let the scrupulous persons converse often of God and with God, but little of themselves, or with themselves. The sentiment of the presence of God, a taste of His sweetness, the luster of His light will dilate their heart, and dissipate that darkness which a gloomy timidity casts over their mind. God is all light, and man is but darkness. When we consider only ourselves, if we expect to find anything but confusion, we might as well look for it in the midst of a dark night. If we must consider self (and it is true we are sometimes to do so with discretion) let us always do it in God, draw near to him, and you will be enlightened; and darkness will only overtake you in proportion as you turn back to self. The pillar which enlightened the Israelites was darkness to the Egyptians; the light of the divine countenance made the difference.

16.

I know not how it can be that scrupulous souls do not turn their delicacy of conscience against their very scruples which often cause them to abandon Communion, and still oftener render their Communions dry, and almost entirely unfruitful. Your confidence in your director is lost, or only resorted to in the last extremity. Confession becomes a torture, and never approached but with trembling, and when you come out from it, it is a criminal who quits the judgment seat. Whilst others progress in virtue, your precious time is lost in tormenting yourself, in weighing atoms, and making monsters of trifles. Almost all the fruit you draw from your piety is to distress your confessors, afflict your friends, and grieve the Spirit of God in you, added to which the health is destroyed, and the mind weakened.

Besides the evil you do to yourself, much is done to others. Piety is rendered disgusting and ridiculous to those who know it not, and think that your uncertainties, your troubles, your torments, and as they call them trifling nonsense is the whole fruit of it. If you still would justify your scruples, I will only ask you if virtue destroys itself.

17.

Have you always found your reproaches and uncertainties of conscience reasonable? A hundred times over you have found them imaginary or absurd. Would it not be excess of imprudence to follow a guide so subject to mislead himself, and mislead you with him, in preference to those who have never misled you?

18.

Your directors have grace and authority to guide you, and your scrupulous conscience has neither the one nor the other. All its authority consists in obliging you to resist it, and the grace you should ask of God is to preserve you from its deceptions.

19.

You say that your confessors cannot see what passes within you, or understand the testimony given by your conscience. Why do you not add that it is surprising Almighty God shall have established them the judges of what they cannot know. Do you really expect to know yourself? This would be deceiving your own heart, which looks too near and is too much interested to be its own judge; but your director is at a proper distance, and as a physician who though he feels not the malady of his patient, yet can judge by his symptoms, knows their effect better than the sufferer himself.

But still, this testimony of conscience which so much alarms you, and occasions your embarrassment with your directors, is it exact; sure to be relied on? You dare not say it is. But the decision of your directors is, and you cannot deny it. It remains only for you to determine why you trust to that which is uncertain and unsafe, rather than to that which is secure and certain.

20.

I have said already, and it cannot be too often repeated: Obedience is the sure and almost only remedy of the scrupulous. It should be ready, resolute, and steady; the fruit of entire confidence not of despotic authority, submitting the mind as well as the heart; otherwise the remedy will be worse than the evil — not that you should use reasonings or arguments with the scrupulous. Instead of dissipating their doubts, this would but increase them, by strengthening their habit of subtilizing and discoursing, and seeking to be convinced, instead of submitting and obeying.

Obedience should be their daily bread; but reasoning rarely used and only when it can be applied with success, as seasoning to nourishment to prevent distaste. Patience in listening to them, condescension to their explications as far as they can be understood (and often you may understand them better than they can themselves) with mildness and compassion; convincing them that their guides are sufficiently enlightened and zealous to conduct them ought to be to them in the place of the most exact and conclusive reasoning.

21.

That submission of mind which the scrupulous should pay their directors ought to extend not only to the belief that they can decide their doubts, but also that they themselves can decide for themselves on such principles as are pointed out to them when they are required to do so. By this means, much labor is abridged for the confessor. The precious time claimed by many penitents and engrossed by these scrupulous souls who would deprive them of it is saved; it is at the same time the best method of treating them, and would eventually cure them if they would persevere in the use of a remedy so little to their taste. The proper time to exact from them an obedience so painful in its practice but useful in its effects, will be known to their director after they have been made to pass through trials less severe and are mutually well known to each other.

22.

To render obedience more consoling, and also more useful, persuade yourself firmly that it is absolutely necessary; that it is to the will of God you should subject yourself, and that He consequently will never impute to you any blame for what you may have done through Christian obedience to an enlightened director. This is an unchangeable maxim; we will explain it. Scrupulosity is an evil, a great evil. It is yours. God Himself who desires your cure provides your remedy, and obedience is that remedy; the only one to be relied on. These principles are undoubted, established by all authors who have treated the subject, many of whom have been acknowledged as saints, and no further discussion is necessary. From whence I draw this conclusion: If God wills you to be cured of your scruples, and if obedience is the sure means, God necessarily wills you to subject yourself, and whatever you do in obedience to your confessors will be an accomplishment of His will.

Consequently, if it were possible that they (the confessors) should be mistaken in their derision of your doubts, you could not make a mistake by following their counsel, and the goodness of God. Even His justice is engaged not to impute to you any mistakes into which you may be led by this religious deference to their authority, since it could be but an innocent, not a sinful mistake as you follow the established order of God, and do not follow your own will in which sin consists, but His, which is the sovereign rule of right; nor the bent of your own inclination which draws you, but that of reason and prudence; nor the persuasions of your scruples which it would be much easier for you to follow than to resist; and you obey in order to conquer, not to please yourself.

23.

Although this reasoning seems clear and conclusive, yet let it be put in another point of view to make it, if possible, still more clear to the scrupulous, to whom even the most evident things are dark, if they are not conformable to their own ideas. The laws of God and of man are obligatory of themselves; but in practice they must be applied by conscience which is the practical judge of reason and dictates its conduct when it is well disposed. These laws are always the same, but not always of equal obligation; nor is it always equally sinful to transgress them because they are not always judged by a conscience equally correct.

Invincible ignorance, a good and sincere intention, will excuse the sin of the transgressors of any law divine or human, because they are unconscious of it. Also, as says St. Bonaventure, *"A free conscience often saves him who merits to be condemned,"* (that is to say, those who do actions in themselves worthy of damnation) because it does not at that moment dictate to him the law which he transgresses; and on the contrary, *too rigid a conscience will sometimes damn the person who deserves to be saved*, because he does nothing to damn himself, but omitting to do what conscience proposes to him as obligatory, though not in itself his actual duty.

If, then, a scrupulous person, agitated by some perplexity on account of certain duties which he/she fears not to have fulfilled, after having proposed their doubts to an enlightened director and done what he prescribes without hearkening to these doubts, on the universally received principle that scrupulous persons should always submit their doubts to obedience, and by so doing, they follow the rule which is prescribed by conscience. Consequently, if the director was deceived, they would be exempt from all sin, because they act according to conscience.

It would be useless to say that conscience has proposed to them to fulfill such a duty, because it has not proposed it as a certain obligation but as a simple fear; and this fear, says St. Bonaventure, is not the dictate of conscience which is the immediate rule of our actions. This fear, far from being a dictate, is not even a real doubt; a doubt admits of *for* and *against* with equal reasons on both sides; instead, this fear is but an uncertainty of the soul for which often it cannot give any reason, or at least whose reasons are evidently destroyed by others which oppose them.

This matter, then, ought to be specially considered by the scrupulous, and carefully distinguished, for quite often, this person imagines a thing to be a doubt which is only fear. I may venture to say that it is often not even a fear of the mind which ought always to have at least some motive, but a mere impression of fancy like that of a child in the dark for which it can give no other reason than fear itself and the darkness.

Thus, we may say, "they fear where no fear is" (Ps 13) and to the greatest extreme without knowing why. Therefore, if they would be but moderately reasonable, they might be easily persuaded that fear without foundation is folly, and more a subject of their pity than their reflection; if docility is added to reason, this impression will be resisted and banished from their mind. When the fear is really founded, and even extends to a doubt, the scrupulous person should always obey and be assured that in so doing, they will be without reproach; even supposing the duty which they fear to have neglected is really unfulfilled, because this doubt is only an uncertainty of the mind, not a judgment of conscience and that this judgment should be the rule of our actions. Reason presents this doubt not as a light to guide it, but a subject for its obedience, and by obeying it follows the last judgment of its conscience, and by following also the direction of its guides, it acts not only by obedience, but also by conscience, *decided* and *reasonable,* opposed to a conscience scrupulous and uncertain.

24.

Let us follow this reasoning still further to render it, if possible, still more evident. We are not always obliged to do what is most secure; what approaches us most to the law of God, and keeps us further off from sin; but only what appears most suitable, most reasonable and most agreeable to Christian prudence. This virtue has a right over us so absolute, although so mild and gentle that it subjects even conscience itself which is the guide of our actions only as far as prudence directs it. Now both reason and prudence direct the scrupulous person by the voice of the saints and most holy writers that they can do nothing better than obey, despite their fears and doubts. Therefore, in obeying, they act wisely, prudently and irreproachably when, in truth, by a mistake of the confessor, and by the purity of their obedience, they may have set aside the law.

Whatever you do in good faith, and with a perfect intention, even should it be itself against the law of God, instead of being a sin, it may well be a good action, if it is done with a good intention. Therefore, as you do your actions in entire faith by the dictates of your director, not from culpable ignorance, carelessness of dissipation or from an erroneous inclination, but from an incontestable maxim proposed to us as the best and only secure rule by the most holy writers, and the dictates of prudence. Perhaps, because of this, you do not sin; on the contrary, you merit before God by your obedience even though by your actions you may have offended against His law.

This reasoning is so common in spiritual writers that it is useless to cite any example; besides in itself it is so clear that it wants no authority to support it. A person who in contradiction to his own will, and without intention, should innocently transgress the law of God by yielding to lawful authority may confidently say to God, "Lord, would you strike the soul of your servant in its ignorance which proceeds from its simplicity and obedience not from its negligence or indifference?"

25.

Be then obedient, but that is not enough. It is even very little, if you are not at peace in your obedience. If you are not submissive in mind as well as your will, if you give up your doubts without forgetting them and leaving them at the feet of your confessor, if you carry them with you in order to present them again in the tribunal, in your next confessions, or if without daring again to present them because they will not be listened to, you listen to them yourself and secretly sigh for your want of conviction, whilst your Lord presents to you the sacred light of the most secure authority.

In short, if you obey like a slave, more from necessity than desire; less by deference and acquiescence to the authority which directs you, than from fear of the excesses into which the indulgence of your scruples may lead you; besides the imperfection of your obedience, you nourish within yourself the evil that devours you, and continue in the same danger of falling in the sorrowful excess in which your scruples would betray you.

Be then tranquilly submissive, and not painfully subjected. Forget these doubts which dry up your soul, and trouble your interior spirit. Examine no more these which have been derided by enlightened prudence. *Walk always forward.* Returning continually on your steps is the means of never advancing; enclosing oneself in a round of perplexities is to renounce all hope, and continually increase our pains. Repose peaceably in Him who offers you every certainty and security in the faithful guidance of His *ministers.*

26.

You are not permitted to repair your past confessions, nor to explain the present ones to your satisfaction. This is only in order to shorten your pain; to afford you as much security of conscience, as repose of mind. Even should these confessions be of as much consequence as you imagine, and you endeavor in vain to persuade your confessor of their importance, should they even be null and void from the moment you sincerely and ardently wish to renew them, and you are prevented only by a religious deference to your confessor, should they be ever so mutilated and imperfect, those which you now make include all and is a virtual renewal of them (though you accuse yourself only of some venial faults) and all your sins are remitted.

All good theologians know the reason, since it is well understood that the integrity of confession does not consist in the exactness of the detail of all your sins, so much as in expressing those on which your confessor permits you to dwell. All the rest are virtually contained in the present confession, and remitted at the same time. Now, prudence and discretion require you to obey, and not to overstep their limits, which a lawful certainty has set to your selfish inquietudes and wearisome details.

27.

I carry the question still further, and suppose that after an ordinary confession in which you had acknowledged yourself culpable only of some venial sins since your last confession, and without a clear recollection of those you had omitted, your confessor should send you to Communion without absolution, after you had declared your uncertainty on those you had omitted. What violence would this effort of obedience cost you; what fears of sacrilege!

But what would be your embarrassment and trouble if, in the hour of death itself, if in the very moment of your last agony you find yourself deprived of the last resource of absolution in your sorrowful perplexities! This terrible blow might hasten your last moments and cast you in the very depths of despair; still, this pain would be the fault of your timidity, or your want of instruction; for a soul courageous and well informed will receive with confidence the sacrament of the dying, and depart in peace to the judgment of God without being prepared by the absolution of the priest; knowing that the Sacrament of Extreme Unction in these circumstances has the same effect as the Sacrament of Penance. What I say of the Sacrament of Extreme Unction, many serious theologians have also said of the Holy Eucharist (as is remarked by St. Thomas, *Summa Theol.*, III, q. 79, a. 3).

Therefore, although this Sacrament generally supposes a state of grace in those who receive it, it sometimes in itself produces it, and effaces mortal sin in those who are unconscious of their guilt and firm in faith. Now, there cannot be a stronger proof of faith than that which is shown by a scrupulous soul when it renounces its doubts to the decision of its confessor. It is then an error in him/her to torment themselves with the fear of sacrilege when by his order (even when uncertain of their confessions) they go to Communion without absolution; since acting with faith in the decision of their confessor, and with proper deference of their own will, the sacrament they receive, far from bringing on them a new sin will efface all, even those which are mortal, at whatever time they were committed. Blessed be His holy name!

28.

It will be also a source of peace for the scrupulous, and a means of sparing themselves many pains, if they reflect more on love than fear, of the virtues they should practice, than the faults they commit. I know that there is a proper time for both these subjects, and we cannot advance far in the cultivation of virtue, except vice is first rooted out. But even this is a condemnation to the scrupulous who chiefly are occupied by the feeling and confession of their faults and seldom by the means of remedy, and acquiring the virtues opposed to them. Generally, more time should be allotted to the acquisition of virtue than the destruction of vice. A good habit will always destroy a bad one, but the destruction of the bad one is not always sufficient to form a good one. This maxim is particularly applicable to the scrupulous. The contemplation and love of good rejoices the heart, and fills it with courage and peace; while, on the contrary, a too frequent consideration of our faults produces only timidity, sadness and trouble.

29.

From the love of good necessarily follows aversion to evil and separation from sin, even venial. In this aversion and separation, a scrupulous soul finds great matter of decision on all doubts respecting mortal sins; for as to those which are venial, he/she ought to detest them in general without deciding on them, and humble themselves without much examination on their extent. Rigorous examinations on trifling faults are often a great proof of self-love, and generally are more embarrassing to conscience than productive of fruits in virtue.

This excessive desire to enlighten our doubts — doubts that often occur — relaxes and weakens devotion whose fervor might efface in a moment and without examination those faults which are real, and even turn to profit those which are doubtful. It is, however, a sure maxim, and I believe one of St. Francis de Sales, that we ought not to fear venial sins (which we are in frequent occasion of) too much, as timidity will lead us in continual perplexities which retard us not a little in the path of virtue.

A traveller who walks fast and gains a considerable distance, although he may sometimes stumble, or even go out of his path, is certainly to be preferred to one who goes with so much precaution, that though he makes no false step, yet fears to lift his foot lest he should hurt it against a stone, or raise a dust to blind him, stopping at every path to examine his way and torment himself with the idea of wandering ever so little out of it. We should then fear less the commission of faults, and be more resolute not to commit any with deliberation and will.

A soul firm in the resolution of avoiding even venial sin and never yielding to it with his/her will and knowledge, may say to himself/herself with courage and confidence in order to dissipate the distressing doubts, "I hate sin," and avoid the occasions of it, "and the disposition of my soul is never to commit it, not even the slightest one, and if I fall by weakness, at least, I do not bend under the habit of it."

As to mortal sin, it seems to me I hate it more than all the evils in the world and the greatest of all my fears is the dread of falling in it, which is a certain proof to me that I really hate it. What then have I done on this occasion which causes my trouble? If I am culpable, it can only be of some negligence, or weakness without reflection; nor does it appear that I have given full consent to a crime. No one passes from one extreme to another, from a great care of salvation and even of perfection to a direct revolt against God and into mortal sin: it is only by degrees we fall into this abyss. We slide sometimes very rapidly, it is true, but still we only slide, and do not plunge in it, but descend from Jerusalem to Jericho. There can be no mortal sin without a deliberate consent, and I have every reason to believe that if I had had liberty of reflection on this occasion, mortal sin would have been as horrible to me as it is at this moment.

30.

This reflection may contribute much to the tranquility of a soul who considers only the past; but for those who consider the present as relative to the past, as for example the doubts they may have of having fulfilled certain duties, and if they ought not to be reconsidered, as to which doubts are the greatest torment of the scrupulous, and which they may clearly decide themselves in this manner. There is nothing I would not be ready to suffer rather than offend God, especially mortally. Had I to do again, not once, but a hundred times that duty I fear to have neglected, I would make no hesitation between that and the greatest of all misfortunes — the loss of God — so that my not doing it again is not from unwillingness to bear the trouble of it, but from the desire to avoid scruple. It is not from laziness since I do what is more painful in many ways and not of obligation; it is not indifference for God, since my sovereign great and only desire is to be wholly His; it is zeal for His service and His love, which meets no greater obstacles than the interior pains I endeavor to surmount.

These fears of not having done my duties well are not felt for the first time, but are old impressions — not lights but troubles. Many times I have been told to despise them and should have done so without being told, since I cannot find in them the *Yes*, or the *No*, in simplicity before God, from His invariable light, but only the uncertainty and darkness of human ignorance; yet the light of my reason and the authority which commands me to follow it speaks to me that *Yes*, which is invariable and which alone can quiet my uncertainties and unite me to Christ Jesus by giving peace to my soul.

31.

These reasonings ought not to be used on all occasions, nor even very frequently (as by them the scrupulous are confirmed in their habit of reasoning with their fears and doubts, which is the source of all their trouble), it is sufficient to do so when they are most agitated. Their impression on the soul will influence them even when they are not conscious of it in the course of their conduct which will become more and more firm, reasonable and decided. But except in occasions of particular alarm, they should cut short all calculations and never reason on common pains, as soon as at the first glance they perceive they have done their duty at least in the essential points.

I say at the first point of view, not the first impression, for it is the light of reason which must direct and not the force of impression. In dwelling on these reasonings, you must not stop to answer the objections which the fears of your conscience may suggest with regard to your separation from sin. This must be judged by the majority of your conduct and general dispositions, for separation from sin does not consist in not committing any, but in a sincere desire of committing it no more, in lamenting that we so easily fall in them through weakness, and taking every precaution against them.

To enjoy God, and offend Him no more is the privilege of the saints in heaven; to serve Him and do penance is the business of those on earth. You should be the more encouraged to follow these reflections by the certainty that should you even make too light of the doubts presented to your mind for the reasons here alleged, it would not be in you a culpable crime, but an innocent error, since only the necessity of conquering your scruples and obeying your director induces you to decide for yourself, and if ever a free and liberal judgment of conscience can save, as has been cited from St. Bonaventure, it is on this occasion. Jesus Christ so far from imputing to you as a crime that you have mistaken Him for a phantom in the night, will hold out His hand to keep you from sinking in the waves. Be courageous, then, and resolute, for much strength is necessary to conquer inveterate scruples. But the light, joy, and peace will sensibly be renewed, and take the place of darkness, chagrin and disquietude. They will support your weakness and be the recompense of your labor.

32.

A scrupulous person reading these reflections will say immediately they do not concern them. But whom, then, do they concern, since they certainly relate to persons most frequently occupied by the state of their conscience, seldom tranquil before God, and seldom satisfied on the accomplishment of their duties; persons of a particular manner of thinking at least with respect to their perplexities who are condemned by all the world, who turn against themselves whatever is said to tranquilize them, because they always take things on the side least favorable to themselves and which they never believe to be sufficiently explained, although they have been repeated times without number, and are considered by the most timid as trifling, who do everything the good and virtuous do, yet never think they do it as they do, and when they sin not in actions, think always they sin by thoughts; persons considered by their confessors, their friends and whoever is acquainted with their manner as scrupulous, and yet will not be persuaded that they are so; or who, if they allow it to be so in general, will never allow it when you enter in detail of their actions; persons, in short, always undecided and unbalanced, and whose fancy and ideas vary from one moment to the other. If you obstinately refuse to acknowledge yourself in this portrait, although every one else sees the likeness, it is true the likeness is not for you.

33.

That jealousy of God which pursues an unfaithful soul by His merciful chastisements is sometimes the source of our interior darkness and afflicting doubts; in which case the evil is useful, provided the cause is acknowledged and the remedy applied. These scruples are the just punishment of our infidelities; and the cessation of our infidelities is the remedy. They are hedges with which God encloses our way because He perceives how easily we stray from it. If we go direct to Him and seek Him with our whole heart as the Royal Prophet [David] did, He will lead us in the broad way which is bounded only by His love.

Every day we see persons recalled to seriousness, application and regularity, however dissipated and careless they have been — happy pains which can accomplish in a short time that which prayer, sacred reading, interior warnings, and even the sacraments have not been able to effect in entire years! The remedy is violent but necessary, when others do not succeed. Let those whom God draws strongly to Himself beware how they force Him to the sad necessity of using it, and those to whom He applies it, not stop or seek for rest in attention only to essential duties, since their best and surest measure is *not to pardon themselves anything*, for God will always be angry while Achan retains any part of that which is devoted to the curse (Jos 7:19). Question your own heart before God as [Joshua] the holy leader of the people of God interrogated the wicked Israelites; compel it to declare whatever the spirit of God reproaches it with, and sacrifice without mercy the secret infidelities which are the cause of its pain.

34.

Sometimes, it is not so much our sensible faults which God punishes by interior pains, as some remains of self-love from which He desires to purify us. It is an imperceptible rust and delicate adhesive, which the fire of tribulation (sometimes the most active and penetrating) alone can clear us from. In this case, the best and first thing we can do is to kiss the hand of God which performs on us this painful but salutary operation, and beg of Him to hasten His work, so that we may finally love Him purely, and enjoy the intimate peace of a perfect heart.

35.

Without prejudice to this entire submission to the stroke we receive from the hand of God, we should employ those measures which are commonly used to overcome the scruples we believe to come from Him; for this is His will in the same manner as He desires we should take remedies even for the corporal maladies He sends us for our spiritual good. Besides, it may happen that we should be deceived and believe a scruple to be sent by Providence, which may arise from another principle. The remedies have the same effect as the disease, and equally enter in the way of our sanctification; the same as bitter potions (the regimen and pre-scription of physicians) often make the patient suffer as much, and sometimes more than the malady itself.

36.

If the evil arises from that seducing vice which enchants us with ourselves and causes whatever humiliates to revolt and discon-cert us, the remedy is well known. Have a low sentiment of your virtue and capacity; let your knowledge always vanish before that of others; let your daily faults, ingenuously acknowledged, abate the pride of your heart. Let your former faults carefully meditated confound your presumption: you will gain an ascendancy over your scruples in proportion as you are more humble in your opinion of yourself.

Accustom yourself to consider the corruption of your heart; its infection will no more give you the agitation which troubles, since not seeking to shine in your own eyes, nor those of others, the obscurity of your soul will not produce that honor which terrifies, nor that confusion which is distressing. The uncertainties of your present state from the moment they are accepted as a just punishment for your past offenses, will no longer throw you in sorrowful alarms. You will no longer be frightened by your littleness when you do not desire to measure yourself with anyone, but consider yourself as inferior to all.

Leaving to others the signal favors of heaven, heroic virtues, and great consolations, then the mediocrity of your graces, the multitude of your defects, the aridity of your soul, will not occasion the chagrin which arises from ambition and give birth to sadness. Without possessing those exalted virtues of which you esteem yourself unworthy, you will possess the greatest fruit they produce which is peace of heart, and you will not be in danger of a great evil resulting from our perverseness which is presumption of soul. You will enjoy without trouble and you will be enriched, without danger of losing humility, not like the idle who hate work, but with the lowly who fear distinction.

Perhaps, you will not think this remedy is necessary to you, or suitable to the malady which has attacked you; but besides that, this proves of itself you stand in need of it; you ought to desire to use it because it cannot be otherwise than beneficial to you. The eyes of God rest on the humble, and their luminous rays dissipate our darkness and with it disappear our doubts and perplexities.

37.

When your scruples proceed wholly and entirely from the enemy (and generally he has a considerable share in them) the remedy just spoken of will also be extremely salutary. The chief opposition we should make to the principles of the proud spirit is humility to confound, obedience to disconcert, and prayer to put them to flight, and since he has a great share in all the different kinds of scruples that he excites or arouses, these three means of combatting him ought to be everywhere employed.

38.

Let us conclude by a necessary advice to those who find themselves relieved after a state of long and extreme suffering, which is, to be on their guard against a subtle snare into which many have fallen at the very moment they had but a step more to withdraw them from the abyss. Comparing their present liberty with their slavery, they have found the difference so great that they have been seized with fear; and seeing less danger in severity than relaxation, they fall in the same state of torment as before; their last state becomes worse than the first, because they are no longer scrupulous by temptation and by a weakness of surprise, but by relapse and by reflection.

The great secret to avoid this danger is always to look forward, and never to judge our present exactness by past scruples, but by the law of God, and the doctrine of those who hold the place of God to us. The head will turn if you look down in the abyss from which you come out, and you will run the risk of falling back again. You must not look, while yet on the brink; when out of danger you may cast your eyes back, and, indeed, you should do so, in order to estimate the happiness of your deliverance, to give thanks to God, and to take precaution for the future.

*   *   *   *   *

Prayer for persons troubled with interior pains.

God of love, God of peace, whose delight is to communicate Thyself to tranquil and peaceful souls who listen in silence to Thee, and not to their weak imagination; who yield to the attraction of Thy love, and not to their inclination for scruple; who follow Thy sweet inspirations, and not those of the enemy always turbulent; who are filled with confidence in Thy paternal goodness, and not with excessive fears if having offended it.

My Lord and my God who sees how the enemy of my happiness and yet more of Thy glory prevails in troubling me, and grieving Thy spirit within me as far as he can, by my vain alarms, internal comments and unceasing restlessness. Grant, Almighty God, that calm may succeed this agitation, light to darkness, and peace to trouble. Command now as heretofore Thou commanded the demons to go forth from the bodies of the possessed. Command my imagination, and all the powers of my soul to obey, as Thou commanded the roaring wind and agitated sea.

Arise, Lord, in the center of my soul, and let my enemies be dispersed like smoke. Let the brightness of Thy divine presence pierce the cloud which surrounds me; give serenity to my soul and that intimate peace surpassing comprehension. I beg this peace not for my pleasure, but for Thy glory, not to enjoy the delights of complacency, but to contemplate, adore and praise Thee without impediments, so that Thou may establish your peaceful reign within me during this life, and make me reign happily with Thee during eternity in the next. Amen.

Part III

WHERE THE PROPER MEANS ARE FOUND TO ACQUIRE THIS PEACE

4.

Your first and greatest fear is that God has withdrawn himself from
you because of your faults, & loves you no longer because he looks on you
with the eye of severity. But let me ask you is it only to punish our
sins that God acts in this rigorous manner towards us --- is it not sometimes
and very often to perfect our virtue - this apparent coldness - is it not rather a means
of his providence to root out our self love and confirm us in patience & humility
- to purify our charity, to render us more perfect in the practice of good
works, and make us more conformable to the model of predestination
Our Lord and Saviour ... to enable us to merit a richer crown in heaven,
and draw upon ourselves more abundant graces on earth. the
authority of all the masters of a spiritual life, & the example of all
the saints who have experienced it, should be sufficient to convince us

——— But suppose it is to punish your faults you are treated
with so much severity - I'd even wish you believed it so provided
your persuasion did not trouble you, for I believe truly that in the
beginning of pious dispositions, when the milk of devotion is most
necessary, and dissipation most frequent, you may have reason to think
that your infidelities to God deprives you of this precious milk, or
your actual negligence which leaves your senses open to dissipation
-- I speak not here of that weariness and distaste in spiritual exercise
caused by a bad habit of body, heaviness of the weather, or malice of
the enemy --- persons versed in an interior life easily discern them
and suffer them in patience -- we will speak only of those aridities
which so greatly disturb them, believing them to be the punishment

CHAPTER I

Humility

1.

This virtue which is the foundation of all others is, above all, necessary to acquire interior peace because it mortifies the passions, insensibly weakens them, and finally destroys them as far as they can and ought to be destroyed. It is a short means of attacking them almost all at once; gentle means which breaks them down, as it were, without combatting them, subjects them without effort, and reduces them less by resisting their strength, than by taking it from them; by withdrawing that which nourishes them — that is, the good opinion they have of themselves and wish others to have of them — as we subdue formidable enemies by striking at their vitals instead of engaging by blows.

A soul truly humble is always tranquil. What can trouble it? The praises it receives rather surprises than inflates it; reproach and blame rejoices it instead of dejecting it, and it is glad to find others have the same opinion it has of itself. Calumny, though grievous, such as giving scandal to truth and justice, does not disconcert it. Prosperity does not exalt it; adversity neither weakens nor discourages. It receives, says St. Francis de Sales (Ep. 48, L. 5), pains with gentleness knowing they are merited; prosperity with modesty knowing it is not deserved. It sees the faults of others with regret, but without trouble, remembering its own, and its own with grief, but without impatience knowing its weakness.

The preference shown to others is no affliction to a humble soul because it is always brighter than it wishes, and considers it a favor to be last in all things. So far distant is it from honors and dignities, that it can never be wounded by passing ambition. Its care is so great to be hidden that its darts cannot reach it. If it is unveiled despite its modesty, if brought forward despite its repugnance, if it is exalted despite its opposition, the envious can never deprive it of repose. I will rather join them in endeavoring to undeceive those who have applauded it. In short, the more it is abased, the greater is its contentment, and it finds a perfect repose in the center of its own nothingness.

2.

Happy situation! exalted state! which might indeed be called enviable, if so low a passion could aspire to so great a good. Truly humble soul, as highly exalted in the eyes of Him who singularly delights to put down the proud, and to raise up the humble, as you are lowly and debased in your own, your justice is like the mountains of God whose summit is continually serene, raised high above winds and clouds: While the proud possess nothing less than the rest they seek, being ignorant of the road which leads to it, and continually wandering from the path in which they enter to reach it.

Torn by the combat of multiplied thoughts within; agitated without by their continual efforts to advance, and by the efforts of opposition which repulse them; jealous of the reputation of others, desiring always to increase their own; exciting by their parade the contempt of those whose esteem they desire, and falling through vanity into follies at which they blush, at the very time they reject all applause. The slightest contempt or highest distinctions equally concur to make them unhappy, like [Haman] the favorite of Ahasuerus who, raised to the highest place near the throne, and to the familiarity of the Prince, sighed without ceasing for the ruin of Mordechai who sat among the guards at the gate of the Palace, and not being able to effect it, he wears away with sadness and even dissolves into tears (Est 6:23).

In short, while the heart of the proud is like a sea agitated by a rough tempest, according to the words of the Holy Spirit (Is 57:20), the humble of heart enjoy a perfect calm, the precious gift of a God faithful to His promises (Mt 11:26).

CHAPTER II

Mortification

1.

Mortification is as necessary to interior peace as humility, and perhaps even still more, as occasions of sensuality recur oftener than those of pride. The life of the senses is entirely opposed to the life of the interior, and whatever is granted to the indulgence of the one will be sure to impair the other. The body and the mind, nature and virtue; the love of God, and love of self mutually balance each other; and as one is lowered the other rises; they are powerful enemies. Whatever fortifies the one destroys the other. The senses give much trouble to a soul who desires to limit them to true necessity, but much more to one who grants them all they covet. The eye is never satisfied with seeing, nor the ear with hearing; they draw us out incessantly to entertain us with exterior things which are always following us when we wish to enter within ourselves. Thus, the senses keep us in continual commerce with creatures which greatly interrupt that which we desire to have with God.

Pleasure holds the soul attached to the earth, and hinders it from rising to heaven; it also impairs its power and weakens it, so as to render it timid and fearful like a child stopped and checked by the smallest thing. On the contrary, mortification renders us vigorous, firm and unshaken. Besides, the enemy who is so terrible to the weak, and is weakness itself to the strong, fears to commit himself with a mortified soul with whom he generally comes off the loser; but he considers with contempt piety itself and even the best resolutions of a sensual soul whose overthrow he is sure of when he pleases, or at least of stopping its progress in virtue, unless by an interference they do not deserve, Almighty God withholds them from falling into crimes. This destroyer of our souls has but two ways of entering in and disturbing them, which are vain glory and pleasure. These being closed against him, he is quite powerless, and we can easily resist him, as those who in a strong fortification behold their enemy going round about them without fearing his insults.

2.

But it is not enough to renounce pleasure. We must also love sufferings; the one only separates us from vice; the other forms us to virtue, and gives us that strength which a mere forbearance from pleasure can never bestow in itself. Spiritual labor fortifies the soul as bodily labor gives strength and health to the body. A person unexercised in austerity and labor is as little capable of solid virtue as a weak and delicate woman is of the painful employments of a rustic. Everything inconveniences her, everything stops her, the smallest exertion puts her out of breath. She quickly seeks to rest herself, true emblem of a soul unused to suffering. Everything agitates, everything vexes her, and deprives her of that peace of soul reserved to men of good will, that is, to those whose resolution is firm and courageous, making them capable of suffering all things.

That peace, like the peace of nations, is the fruit of war, and if the labors of the one are not endured, the repose of the other cannot be enjoyed. It is the unction of the Holy Spirit which tranquilizes and sweetens our interior; it is the knife of mortification which makes this balm flow over our souls. Even when this sensible unction is wanting, the power of mortification will support and enable us to combat through the night with the wind and waves until the Savior returns (Mt 14:25). The peace it bestows is less sensible, but more solid, because it will proceed from the depths of a soul resigned and contented with whatever God wills, and truly peaceful although agitated in external motion, as the hull of a vessel may be still, though the rigging and sails are shaking in the wind. In this state of trying agitation, and *insensible peace*, we believe ourselves in excess of misery, while in reality we are rich before God who crowns that soul with benediction, who hides itself in the incorruptibility of modesty and tranquility of spirit.

Those who imagine that there is nothing but consolation in the practice of virtue are in great illusion. It is generally that of beginners who with the sons of Zebedee request of our Lord the tranquil delights of His Kingdom. But what does our Savior say to them? "Can you drink of the chalice of which I drink?" Can you suffer, and suffer in every way, within and without, in body and soul, in sickness and temptation, in contradiction with mankind, in weariness with yourself, in war with demons, in trials from the Lord? If you are resolute to suffer all that, you will enjoy a fund of peace as inexhaustible as the depths of the sea, or like the waters of a great river which flow without ceasing, and never are dried.

Perhaps, heretofore, you have only sought the sweetness of piety, and therefore it has been so unequal, because its delights are not always lasting. You were devout by intervals because your devotion was sensual. You desired, as says Saint Francis de Sales (Ep. 48, L. 5) to pray in the water of Nafe, and to be virtuous in eating sugar. As soon as your spiritual exercises lacked the seasoning of sweetness, and your prayers were no longer perfumed, you became sad and discouraged, and your sensual self forced you to seek in creatures the pleasure you were denied in commerce with God, and peace and recollection is lost.

To regain them you must be again indulged with caresses, and perhaps become still more delicate; the smallest occasions of suffering by the interior contest they occasion, again drive them away. You abandon your spiritual exercises or perform them negligently; one day, you leave them, as says St. Teresa, because your head aches, the next because it has ached, and the third for fear it should ache again. These weaknesses were supportable in your spiritual infancy, but it is time to show that you are older, and stronger, and intend in future to possess your soul in patience, in unwearied patience, because crosses are sown all over by the merciful hand of a God who knows their value and use, and that those who desire to be a moment without suffering will never possess a solid peace.

Chapter III

Fidelity to our exercises

I have just now mentioned a subject of too much importance to be passed over in a slight manner, namely, fidelity to spiritual exercises. It should be great, because the slightest neglect weakens the spirit of the interior and consequently the peace of the soul. It is necessary that this exactness should be perfect, for without it everything will be confusion. We become relaxed, dissipated, weak and insensibly estranged from God. Every desire is indulged, and we only become sensible of our danger when we are already plunged in it so far as to have no hope of withdrawing from it. It is easy to see in the history of all the first and great masters of a spiritual life, and the maxims of the Saints that nothing is so strongly recommended as this exactness, especially to beginners, and even the most perfect, far from relaxing from it, have made it the most essential duty and even a sort of holy slavery.

They considered their practices of piety as so many ramparts to cover their important duties and assure their salvation. And with this intention, they augmented their number as much as possible to keep their enemy at a greater distance and oblige him to make his assaults in a manner less advantageous to him, and more secure for them. The example of some saints who have carried their rigidity to excess on some occasions sufficiently prove its necessity. Yet, without a particular attraction from the common path, we must never venture to depart from it, but must learn to yield with prudence to necessity and propriety. Inflexibility and obstinacy dishonor piety, render it troublesome to our neighbor and generally proceeds from self-love. They are in direct opposition to interior peace which requires that pliancy which carries off all exterior hindrances, without noise or opposition. We must bend without resistance, without vexation, without chagrin to whatever charity, humanity and reason require of us at the expense (if necessary) of our rule of conduct.

But let us beware of relaxing too easily which would no longer be a compliance but a dissipation. Where the spirit of God is, there is liberty but not licentiousness. Let us be simple and pliant, but strong and consistent. As to the rest, exactitude in personal and particular practices should never constrain the interior attraction of peace and recollection, since the one is so necessary to the preservation of the other.

Chapter IV

Moderation of fervor

We must then acquit ourselves of our pious exercises with fidelity — but not with the fervor acquired by our own efforts, which is less a fervor of the soul, than of the body and mind. Whatever is added to that divine movement which comes from God alone, and our own fidelity is foreign to true devotion and contrary to peace of soul.

Let us fulfill the duties of piety in their time and proper extent, with external modesty and internal reverence, with an attentive spirit and an obedient willing heart, *leaving to God the care of all the rest*. Nor must we be uneasy with regard even to those dispositions, or scrupulously seek for them in ourselves since the inquiring into them will rather indulge self-love than be pleasing to God.

Let us unite zeal with holy liberty and we will serve God not with the formality of a proud debtor who desires to be acquitted and to owe nothing, nor like an unhappy slave who serves a severe master, but with the attention and freedom of a docile loving child, who *serves a tender father*.

Our fidelity with regard to time and extent of duty, ought not to be geometrically measured, but simply: the exterior modesty composed, not constrained or affected; our respect humble and simple, not depressed; the attention of the mind consists not in freedom from distraction but in not yielding to them with reflection; our attention of heart not sensible, *but effective*. These observations would certainly suffice to exclude whatever might interrupt our spiritual repose by the indulgence of misplaced zeal and fervor ill understood, if the excessive anxiety which many give themselves to stop the progress of their distractions and to excite the affections of the heart, if their great uneasiness when they do not succeed did not oblige us to extend the subject on two points so interesting in a spiritual life.

CHAPTER V

Patience in distractions

We must, no doubt, as far as it depends on us, employ all the attention of our mind in prayer, in meditation and every pious exercise which requires interior application, but without fear of the distractions which may come to us, without uneasiness when they come, and without alarm when they are past. It is nearly the same thing with respect to attention as intention; they subsist in the same action until they are revoked voluntarily. Whatever wanderings the mind may have made, we are always attentive until our distractions have been willful and with reflection.

Let us apply ourselves without expectation of being settled; the instability of our mind is incapable of it, but on the contrary, becomes irritated and often wandering in proportion to the efforts made to restrain it. It will sometimes remain quietly enough with us; but only the effort to keep it, is sure to drive it away. Let us neither think of it or its distractions, and then we will be attentive. The straining of our imagination will only be a useless fatigue to the brain, destruction of the health to no purpose, and certain interruption of the peace of the soul. It is aiming at impossibility, and a folly to expect to rule it by force; it would be as easy to shut the air in our hand by closing it, as to fix the imagination by constraining it; for should we succeed to drive away every other object for a moment, it would be then occupied by the constraint itself.

CHAPTER VI

Tranquility in our actions

1.

The heart is slower, and more capable of being fixed than the mind and imagination, but its movements also are less perceptible, and therefore, more difficult to be known by those who wish to execute their affections strongly. Its nature is very little known by those who imagine they can discern its action by that of the body, and believe they love because they are softened — for this tenderness is only of the blood and organs, which are far from being the seat of sacred love.

All is gentle and moderate in the service of God. He neither desires us to weary our head, or exhaust our breast by our ill-timed efforts, and consequently, we should neither torture our minds to subject their inconstancy, nor keep our hearts under a pressure to bring forth their affections. These motions would not produce the desired effect because the heart requires to be free and unrestrained. What is sometimes taken for love of God and zeal for His service is neither the one nor the other, and we obtain nothing but illusion of mind, from the torment we have given our body and soul.

Is it truly the love of God we seek in all these efforts? No, it is our own satisfaction. God only asks of us a solid preference, a uniform conduct, and tranquility of soul, peaceful submission to the orders of His providence, an attentive not an eager zeal for the fulfillment of its known will to which we will limit ourselves, if we seek only Him. When we have told a friend that we sincerely love him, and all we have is at his disposal, that we are ready to sacrifice ourselves for him, we are satisfied with ourselves, and have reason to think he is also, although we gave him this assurance in a simple tone, without animated gestures, looks of fire, convulsive moments, and shortened respiration, and that because we know natural expressions and ingenuous manners are the true language of the heart, and it is only our heart [that] our friend requires of us. Do we think that God demands more? Did He ever say to us, "Give me your head, or your breast, your hand or your eyes"? Give Him your heart, it is all He asks, and remain in peace.

2.

But still further, we ought to repress with gentleness these sensible emotions even when they come to us without our efforts. These interior boilings of heated imagination, and sallies of natural activity, and often of presumption, only fill us with ourselves, and inflate our devotion.

"It is," says the Apostle St. Peter, "a foreign [strange] fervor which only leads us astray, and is a real temptation to us" (1 P 4:12). Our joy in this world should be in participating in the sufferings of Jesus Christ, and our consolation in experiencing the anguish of His agony. He will give us a full payment of holy ardors, pious transports and delightful effusions of the fires of divine clarity when He manifests His glory in the heavenly Jerusalem.

If He sometimes visits our hearts with some small portions of it in this valley of tears, it is only passing, and when He sees proper, not willing us either to wish for it anxiously, or to desire its enjoyment. Whatever we do to attract it will be fruitless, and whatever our efforts may produce will be a deceiving imitation, which will only produce the flattery of self-judgment.

In truth, during these moments of ardor, we imperceptibly admire the beauty of our thoughts, the strength of our courage, the veracity of our emotions, and become quite proud of the fine rust which covers us: as soon as we perceive it, the only remedy we have is to let all these movements subside of themselves and to hide ourselves in God, keeping ourselves in His divine presence in humble silence, looking on Him from time to time with modesty and respect.

3.

He will give us these peaceful movements when He sees proper, and does not desire our efforts when they disturb the peace of the soul which He so much desires. We must wait for them — not anticipate them; *we must follow after, not go before Him*, and in this our chief glory should consist. It is in vain, says [David] the Royal Prophet; you rise before day, and work in darkness; sleep in peace till the sun shall appear, and bring with it light, heat and motion.

Nourish yourself, in the meanwhile, with the bread of compunction to fortify and sustain, and with the water of tears, which quiets and tranquilizes: In the midst of this interior sleep, and when you least expect it, the heavenly Spouse will come, and introduce you in the festal chamber, where the delights you will taste in this miserable exile will give you a comprehension and desire of those which He prepares for you in the celestial beatitude, which is the inheritance of the Lord, and the recompense of His children.

Then you will discern the motions of grace from those of your own creation; you will comprehend and feel the truth of what you now believe, that no one can go to Christ except the Father draw him. God will do more in one moment than you could do in your whole life. "You will walk," says the Lord, "in ways that you know not, and shall advance with rapidity, as the darting of an arrow from the bow of a strong man" (Ps 126). This is what God does when He pleases, and what we may hope for, if we are faithful, and what we should neither anticipate by our impatience, nor trouble by our efforts. We must not then repress all sensible and lively motions of the interior.

There are some to which we should yield ourselves without reserve. Many marks are to be given by which they may be discerned, but it is sufficient now to observe that they are to be connected with tranquility in God who is the author of them, and who having formed us in His image, desires us to imitate Him in our conduct, and resemble Him as far as our weakness permits in a continual activity, and a perfect repose.

Chapter VII

Suffer without inquietude the aridities of the soul

1.

Far from seeking to excite a sensible enjoyment in our pious affections, we must patiently suffer aridities and disgusts, and always give the preference to solid peace rather than to passing consolations arising either from natural feelings, or reluctantly granted to our excessive weakness. In truth, it is commonly only weak souls, little versed in interior life, who seek for consolations with ardor, and afflict themselves in aridity.

As soon as God ceases to caress them as a tender mother caresses her little child at the breast, they think they are abandoned by Him and are tempted in their turn to abandon Him. Generally, they neglect His service, and always lack their peace of heart. This evil is so common that the most spiritual books fully treat of it, and from them I will draw only what is necessary to my subject.

In the first place, I acknowledge that it is sorrowful, indeed, to fulfill the most sacred duties of piety with a cold heart, dissipated mind, returning to them always without zeal, obliged as it were to drag the heart by force remaining before God without feeling, in stupid indifference, praying without recollection, meditating without affection, confessing without sorrow, communing without enjoying, eating the celestial bread with less satisfaction than the material, suffering without internal comfort, carrying heavy crosses, without the secret unction which sweetens them, but rather enduring hidden ones more weighty than those which appear.

This situation is without doubt very mortifying, but provided with much wisdom by the providence of God who perfectly knows our wants and necessities. You are just, O my God! and your decrees are dictated by truth itself, but your mercy is never separated from your counsels and directs all your ways. Who shall enter into judgment with you?

2.

Either it is to punish your faults, or to augment your merits that God withdraws His consolations. If it is to punish your faults, why do you not turn your discontent against yourself? If it is to increase your merits, why complain of Him? If He treats you as you deserve, what wrong does He do you? If He desires to give you more than you deserve by giving you more occasions of merit, what gratitude do you not owe to Him? Do you fear that He will either make you expiate your sins too easily in this world, or by a slight suffering render you too happy in the other? Whatever may be your reasoning, what you call His rigor has one of these two motives: God does not hate His own work, and does not call men to His service to render them more wretched. Always happy in Himself, He has not created them in His own image to enjoy the pitiful satisfaction of seeing them miserable in it. Nor yet to draw them with one hand, and repel them with the other by sporting with their weakness. He sports with the heavens and the earth and the elements which He changes at His will without changing, however, the first order of His providence.

As for man, God guides him with a care which proves that in him He respects the image of His divinity itself, keeping in view the glorious end for which He created him; His word which He has given him; the adoption to which He has elevated him; the favors with which He has crowned him; His love with which He has cherished him; and the blood of Jesus Christ with which He has covered him.

If, then, He chastises you, love Him; if He works to your perfection, love Him still more, because He shows you the greater love. If He makes you sensible of your slightest failings, be not troubled. It is a proof He desires to save you; if He puts you to the severest trials, be troubled still less, since it is a proof He wishes to make you a saint. There is nothing then in interior aridities which should give you trouble and dejection, much less tempt you to murmuring impatience.

3.

This is enough to stop the complaints of these sensual Israelites who are disgusted with the sterility of the desert, and tempted to return into Egypt. Now we must draw those from their error who think they are not in the promised land, because the manna does not fall. That which troubles and afflicts me (says each of these good souls, more fearful than impatient) is the uncertainty of these ways in which I walk. I should be satisfied if I did but walk with God. I know His sovereignty, and my own dependence that He merits the purest love, and may justly exact the most painful services; but what destroys my confidence, and with it the peace of my soul, is the fear that God has withdrawn Himself from me because of my sins, or because I serve Him so ill; I fear that He loves me no more, since He never looks on me but with a severe eye; or that I love Him no more myself, since I consider Him with so much coldness.

Souls of little faith and consequently far from interior peace (because it is only found in the obscurity of night by the light of a lively faith) these are your fears, and here are my reflections. You acknowledge the justice due to God, but you allow none to yourself. You submit yourself to His power, but you are not penetrated with His love and goodness; you are very ready to conceive what He requires of your fidelity, but are unconscious of His desire to support your weakness. You know not yourselves, nor your own infirmity; neither the favors which God gives you, nor their effect upon you.

Is it a false humility which makes you fear to perceive in yourself the smallest gift of God? Is it through humility you make it a merit to torment yourself on the accomplishment of your duties, so that the least repose seems a loss to your good works? Is it through secret presumption you believe that you may do a great deal for the service of God, and that devotion and fervor are at your own disposal? Is it by presumption that you are so much occupied with yourself that you can never be satisfied with your actions, because you are solicitous about them? I know not which of these sentiments causes your uneasiness? Perhaps a want of instruction more than either; therefore, let us pass on to further considerations.

4.

Your first and greatest fear is that God has withdrawn Himself from you because of your faults, and loves you no longer because He looks on you with the eye of severity. But let me ask you, is it only to punish our sins that God acts in this rigorous manner toward us? Is it not sometimes and very often to perfect our virtue? This apparent coldness — is it not rather a means of His providence to root out our self-love and confirm us in patience and humility, to purify our charity? To render us more perfect in the practice of good works, and make us more conformable to Jesus Christ, our Lord and Savior, the model of predestination, to enable us to merit a richer crown in heaven and draw upon ourselves more abundant graces on earth. The authority of all the masters of a spiritual life and the example of all the saints who have experienced it, should be sufficient to convince us.

But suppose it is to punish your faults that you are treated with so much severity by God. I could even wish you believed it so, provided your persuasion did not *trouble* you; for I believe truly that in the beginning of your pious dispositions, when the milk of devotion is most necessary, and dissipation most frequent, you may have reason to think that your infidelities to God deprive you of this precious milk, or your actual negligence which leaves your senses open to dissipation.

I speak not here of that weariness and distaste in spiritual exercises caused by a bad habit of body, heaviness of the weather, or malice of the enemy. Persons versed in an interior life, easily discern them and suffer them in patience. We will speak only of those aridities which so greatly disturb them, believing them to be the punishment of their faults, and which they consider as a mark of abandonment by God.

But what faults are those which your fears so much exaggerate? A simple pleasantry followed up too far; an innocent conversation too much prolonged; a lawful opening of the heart, but too excessive; a pleasure not forbidden but unnecessary, allowed to your senses; an infidelity to the attraction of grace, or to your exercises; too long an absence from the remembrance of God or your own interior; an action done out of time by a natural desire or too great eagerness? Is it for such faults that He who is *all love* and abandons even the greatest sinner with regret, and only as it were, by force abandons you?

Is this reason sufficient for His reprobating you, or for you to yield yourself up to discouragement and almost to despair?—Ah! This disposition of yours indeed offends His goodness; sometimes, more than any fault you can commit. Surely, you should reflect that often it is the goodness of God itself which makes you sensible of the faults you commit, converts them to a means of merit, and even occasions of virtue. He commanded the Israelites to wander in the desert for forty years because of their indocility and revolts, but He made use of all this time to lead them to perfection by strengthening their faith, exercising their patience, teaching them to estimate those goods after which they had long sighed, and the ceremonies and practice of His laws in the most detailed manner.

While He punished them with some severity, He protects and defends them in the most striking manner. He guides them Himself through the vast desert, walking always before them, instructing them by His word, and providing for all their wants, furnishing them with daily bread *from heaven*, drawing them water abundantly from the hardest rocks, preserving even miraculously the clothes which cover them. Such is the God whom we serve. It is thus He loves, even while He chastises us.

The example of one of our most distinguished saints will also instruct you. She being accustomed to speak with religious persons of the sweetness of spiritual exercises, and the great advantages of them, and finding them less versed in this knowledge than herself, she permitted a certain complacency to rest in her heart (as even saints themselves have not always been superior to the emotions of self-love) and for this fault God was pleased to deliver her for several years to interior desolations and aridities more painful than death itself.

You to whom this instruction is addressed, timid and fearful soul, would have thought that God abandoned her without resources; but the saint, who knew the value of this merciful severity, only drew from it new motives of fervor, and confidence turning it so much to advantage, that her fault greatly contributed to her sanctification. Like the spouse in the Canticles, she sought her beloved with a diligence proportioned to the distance He had fled from her, when He found her surprised by the slumbers of night, and her persevering fervor insured her the durable possession of His sweet society.

5.

In the second place, you fear that God has withdrawn Himself from you because you serve Him so ill, and do whatever belongs to His service with an insupportable heaviness, and therefore, have reason to fear He rejects you because of your tepidity? I answer to this that if, indeed, your negligence is voluntary, you have reason to fear, although there is also room for consolation. Renew your fervor with moderation and exactness; awake from this sleepiness, and God will still remain with you, even if He was ready to withdraw Himself.

But if this heaviness is altogether involuntary, if it is still more afflicting to yourself than displeasing to God; if you mourn over it with a real desire that it was changed to fervor, your fears, though they are useful for your humiliation, are really without foundation, and ought not to trouble you; moderate them and all will go well.

This heaviness you feel in your holy exercises is quite natural. God, after giving us the grace of baptism, does not punish us for the defects we bring with us at our birth. Sensible fervor is not in our own power! God alone can give it to us. And if He does not bestow it, will He revenge Himself on us for our want of what He withholds when even through our own fault He withdraws it? If we support the privation with humility and persevering patience as a dry fervor substituted for a fervor of enjoyment, far from rendering us culpable, draws upon us the consolations of God who cannot be insensible to our penitence.

Therefore, we have no reason to lose peace in our affliction, since He who Himself allows it to fall on us has no other thought of us, nor any other views, but those of Peace (Jr 19:21). He desires even more than we do ourselves to see our patience proved, our sins expiated, and sufferings ended. Your state is far from being actually tepid, since you do not neglect yourself, are cautious against even the slightest faults, grieving when you fall in them through frailty, and fulfill the duties of our calling and state of life. Should some neglect be mixed with them, the *eye of love* of Jesus who died for you sees only in this the natural effect of the suffering and constrained state in which you are. Then why do you judge it to be an actual coldness which banishes you from His heart, and forces Him to reject you?

6.

Let us pursue these reflections to calm your heart. You do not love God, do you say? You who for His sake deprive yourself of commerce with the world, the pleasures of the senses, of a thousand conveniences of your condition, and the diversions of your age? You who adore Him, pray to Him, meditate His word and laws? You who look upon His enemies, and the outrages they commit with horror, and with a proportioned delight on those who adore and serve Him with fidelity?

You whose greatest contentment would be to know that you please Him, and whose alarm and uneasiness at your aridities is the fear of displeasing Him? You who serve your neighbor despite your repugnance, because God wills it, and who Himself serves him, notwithstanding your distaste because he merits it.

Does this prove only indifference for God? Has His love any other marks? He crowns you with His favors, and instead of acknowledging them with humility, you pass the time tormenting yourself that you should employ in thanksgiving. Being so fearful of your inactivity in His service, should you not also fear the consequence of your ingratitude? Do you think we can serve Him without His help, or support the labors of that service without His love? Acknowledge with humility the gifts of His love, and abandon yourself freely to the impressions of His grace. Serve Him without so many reflections on your manner of doing it. These are the only distractions you do not fear, though of all others, they are the most hurtful to you. Occupy yourself much with God, and little with yourself.

7.

But your aridities call your attention to yourself in spite of yourself. Yes, and perhaps through self-love more than through devotion. Your pain is that you are displeased with yourself, and you think that it is because God is displeased with you. But if He chooses to conduct you by this way, why do you seek another? Could the one you would choose please Him better, who asks nothing so much as submission to His will, or be more useful to you who want nothing so much as to die to yourself? Leave all to Him; He knows better than you do what is best for you. Do your duty as perfectly as you can, and remain in peace; be contented with what He gives you, since He is willing to be content with what you are able to do for Him.

Chapter VIII

Life of faith

Enter courageously in the life of faith in proportion to the measure with which God attracts you, and walk in it with freedom, never desiring to depart from it. Let His obscurity be your light, and His firmness your support. The cloud of darkness will strike you with horror at first; your inquietude will be perpetual; you will desire, like St. Thomas, to touch and to see. But if you faithfully resist, and resign yourself to see still less, instead of asking for light, if you shut your eyes to the false light of imagination which you are tempted to prefer to more usual darkness, and advance steadily in this obscurity where nothing rejoices your sight or consoles your heart, but the accomplishment of God's will, with the hope of His mercies, an intimate solid peace will be the fruit of your labor and patience. This life of faith is very humiliating. In it, we are compelled, as it were, to lose sight of self, except when obliged to regulate our actions and duties, to purify their intention, and make them meritorious by offering them to God.

This life of faith is also very mortifying, because it deprives us of all sensible support. It banishes those lively images of imagination, which (false as they are) we love to encourage rather than not hold to something. It takes off our attachment to great austerities which are not a part of our duty or attraction, and in which a soul that God is leading to self renunciation seeks a resource; it counts for nothing all sensible enjoyments which are, indeed, less than nothing in those who esteem them to be something.

A soul in this state, deprived of all support, in whom faith alone remains with its obscurities, hope with its uncertainties, and charity still more enveloped in darkness than faith and hope, the fulfillment of common duties without interest in them, peace of heart without any sensible feeling which recalls us to ourselves, a dry meditation on the sacred mysteries of Jesus Christ and the truths of Religion, and absolute forgetfulness of all things of the world, this soul, finding itself, as it were, all alone with God, shudders at this vast solitude; but if it confides in God, if it is content to be possessed of Him alone, how much will it interest that God who is all love, in its sanctification!

How great will be her progress in the ways of spirituality! What peace will be established in her heart! It will be as if suspended in the air and often by this total abandonment to divine providence, like the prophet Habakkuk, carried by a single hair of the head (Dn 14).

But secure it will be in a support apparently so weak! How rapidly will it advance in this unbeaten path, and how much will its celestial spouse feel for her while passing through it (Sg 9)! What can more surely awaken God's pity than this renunciation of all sensible support, to be solely supported by Him! Can anything more fully testify faith in His word, and confidence in His goodness? He who confidently walks in an unknown way, through the thickest darkness, without hesitation, or feeling the way; without sighing after light, or holding by the hand the guide who conducts it, depending as much on his word as on his own eyes, testifying an entire confidence in him and his fidelity. How can we better prove our love to God, or more surely draw His love on us, than by living in the darkness of faith!

Chapter IX
Love of God

1.

It is in this divine love above all things that we shall find interior peace; it is the great means of acquiring it, and all others depend upon it. The soul possessed of its God through love, reposes in Him as its center. In vain it seeks for rest everywhere else. Like a dislocated limb, it suffers everywhere because it is out of place. That fund of inquietude which it always carries within itself is changed to consolation and peace. By agitations and great labors it had brought on itself many troubles, and by small attentions and fidelity to love, it finds its repose and happiness. In proportion as this love augments, its passions become purified, and its peace more intimate and solid. It considers itself in this world as in a desert exile; all appears foreign to it, nothing interests it, nothing attaches. The pleasures of the senses become insipid to it and even insupportable.

Earthly goods appear frivolous and even burdensome. The employments of people of the world are mean and silly in its eyes, if not culpable. Their intrigues, far from being interesting, create abhorrence; their forgetfulness, far from afflicting, consoles it because it leaves the soul entirely to itself and allows it liberty to employ itself with the object of its love.

This occupation, so wearisome to an indifferent soul, is a joy and delightful response. It is no longer wearied by the weight of the body; the miseries of this life no longer plunge it in sorrow and sadness; multiplicity of thought no longer bewilders it; a perfect silence, deep and tranquil, reigns throughout its interior.

2.

The love of creatures is passionate, inflaming, and transporting. The ardor with which it is pursued by man would make it appear that he finds in them the end of all his desires, and the beginning of all fidelity; rather they find nothing else but agitation and inquietude, deceit and disappointment. Experience itself does not always make him wiser, and misfortune only increases his delusion. His desires multiply, and are embittered by every disappointment; one affliction always brings with it the seeds of another. Created things being outside of himself, he is obliged to leave himself to seek them. He is rapidly drawn towards these nothings and obliged to run in order to reach them. If he seizes them, they escape him; if for a moment he enjoys them, besides the fear of loss, he finds in them a void, even while his enjoyment is at its height, because these gross and limited pleasures cannot reach the heart, or fill the soul whose desires are infinite. They cannot be food for an immortal being who may, indeed, forget itself so far as to be amused by them, but they can never serve to nourish it, as the air may fill us but cannot feed or satisfy us. The soul finds God within oneself. Whenever it enters there it is sure to find Him, and in Him his/her *food, strength,* his/her *all.* God's infinity fills man's whole capacity, and in possessing Him it possesses *All.*

It is in vain to represent to someone the opulence and enjoyments of worldings, and his/her comparative poverty. No argument or persuasion can prevail against the certain and positive possession of their own happiness. But one desire remains to them, which is to unite oneself more and more to the only object of their love; but this desire, instead of troubling them, brings calm and peace in the heart, both by hope which accompanies it, and the enjoyment it anticipates and augments.

CHAPTER X

Conformity to the will of God

The love of God produces submission of our will to all the orders of His providence; and our submission preserves us in a holy tranquility amidst the most painful reverses, and an admirable equilibrium of mind through the greatest agitations and most cruel vicissitudes of this life.

If we love God, His divine will, will always be ours, and having no will but His, nothing, not even what is most afflicting, will be contrary to ours, because nothing happens in this world but what He either orders or permits. What happiness for us to unite ourselves with this sovereign providence which arranges, governs and preserves all things!

To will whatever He wills, and to will nothing more; consequently, to be sure of having always what we choose, to suffer only what we desire to suffer, thus we become in a manner the arbiter of our own fate. How elevated! How calm, and how mysterious this peace of the soul! To do always our will because we will not do God's will, to forget ourselves entirely and find ourselves again entirely, as wholly as we had lost ourselves. But because we had lost ourselves for God, we find ourselves in Him.

Is this a fiction of piety? Is it a dream of our imagination? When the divine oracles were silent; when the example of the saints did not prove it, the truly pious soul would be sufficiently convinced; true children of providence, who eat only of His bread, whose thoughts are always on Him, who act only by His direction. That providence carries you as a mother carries her unborn babe. How great is the repose you enjoy! How sweet the rest you find in its bosom! You are on all sides sheltered, as with an impenetrable buckler, from the arrows which fly by night and by day. Either it repels them, or if it permits them to reach you, it assures you they come not from the hand of a pitiless enemy, but from that paternal goodness which never gives a useless wound, and can heal as quickly as it can afflict.

Knowing that not one hair of your head shall fall without His will, *you possess your soul in patience.* I speak not here of your love for the cross because Jesus, our Savior, loved it, and was Himself fastened on it; nor that you will receive afflictions with joy, but you will receive them with a holy diffidence of yourself, because you know their utility, and your own weakness.

Nor do I say that you will receive prosperity with thankfulness but with fear, because it is generally dangerous, and granted only to our spiritual loss. But your tranquility will be perfect under the eye of God who sees all; under His almighty power which can do all; under His guidance which directs all, and specially in the arms of His love where your repose will be divine and indescribable. In you, I love to contemplate what the Saints have taught by their doctrine and example, what the good angels cherish with so much care, and the bad ones regard with so much envy; what the impious blame and what every righteous soul endeavors to imitate.

CHAPTER XI

Frequent Communion

Holy Communion is a source of Peace, since it unites us to Him who ardently desires it should reign in us, and who alone can give what He himself requires of us. Generally, it produces interior calm and a tenderness of sentiment which warns us of the movements of our passions at their very birth, and a sensible force to resist them. There, spiritual sweetness is tasted in its source, moderates the bitterness of the heart and rectifies all its desires. Persons who frequently communicate are seldom governed by their passions or subject to humor and caprice. They are generally peaceable and can master themselves at least to a certain point. If there are some in whom this effect is not seen after frequent communion or at least an habitual endeavor to repress the violent sallies of nature, let them enter within themselves to examine what obstacles they put to the operations of this divine sacrament.

We have already said that interior peace is a disposition for Communion; and here we say, it is the effect of it which should not be considered as contradictory, because it is the same with respect to purity of heart, the love of God, and all other good dispositions which Communion requires, and which it also augments. It is thus one good Communion is a preparation for another, because it increases in the heart the good dispositions which had first disposed it, and produces fruits from every seed of virtue it finds within it.

CHAPTER XII

Mental Prayer

1.

But one of the most powerful means, without which most others either cannot subsist in us, if they do, can produce but a very imperfect effect, is prayer. As soon as we approach to God, we become enlightened. Peace and serenity soon succeed to confusion and darkness, and our sighs to Him will dissipate our sorrows. However disturbed, troubled, or vexed we may be when we enter into prayer, we feel ourselves tranquilized by degrees; if, at the end some pain remains, we must leave with the sweet repose prayer procures us.

The examples of the saints who employed whole nights in this heavenly exercise, or rather seemed never to interrupt it is proof sufficient of its effects and the peace it procures, without which they could not have persevered in it so long a time. An agitated soul being like a person sick with fever, and deprived of sleep, who turns and turns incessantly, it would be for him an insupportable torment to remain in one position.

In the same manner as we judge of the efficacy of remedies, and the decrease of a malady by the tranquility of a patient, so may we judge by the repose of a soul in prayer the decrease of its passions, and its progress in this holy experience.

Whatever may be said of interior peace, and the different methods of acquiring it, prayer must always be the most essential without which neither the means nor the end can be effectual. If some souls are possessed of tranquility without having applied to meditation, and are even ignorant of the theory of it, it is because God gives them a manner of prayer they do not discern, and this prayer is often of a nature the most sublime.

2.

Holy Communion, which in itself contains the Author of all Graces, does not produce peace of soul without prayer, which disposes us for this sacrament by a preparation both distant and immediate, and yields its fruit by the thanksgiving and recollection of mind which follows; prayer which unites it to God, nourishes us with Him, and thereby becomes of itself a sort of sublime and celestial communion, and may even substitute sacramental Communion as we have seen in Saint Magdalene, Saint Paul the Hermit, and Saint Mary of Egypt.

Yet, we are far from desiring to diminish the zeal of frequent Communion among the faithful, but rather would increase it, and inspire the whole world with the dispositions so much wished by the Church itself; we would wish with the Council of Trent (Sess. 22, c.6) that they communicate at every Mass they assist at. Those who are prevented from receiving the sacred Eucharist as often as they wish may supply its want by *Prayer* of which nothing can deprive them but their dissipation and negligence.

Prayer then may substitute for frequent Communion, but only in case of necessity and when we are not deprived of it through our own fault. Those who of their own accord and without necessity would substitute one for the other would yield to illusions, and would with great danger depart from the order of Providence who desires to communicate His graces to us in a special manner by this sacrament. Our Lord seems to have instituted it particularly under the form of daily nourishment, and ordered us to feed upon it, to teach us the hidden secrets of our hearts which are often unknown to us, and to force us, as it were, to enter them at least with Him, and acquire the habit of recollection first in His presence, then in His absence, and at last in a continued tranquility and repose.

A soul in the habit of frequent Communion insensibly acquires a great facility in entering this interior sanctuary and preserving its peace in this profound solitude where at one time it enjoys the presence of our Lord and at another adores the place where His feet stood in a former Communion, and prepares itself in the best manner it is able for the one it anticipates.

CHAPTER XIII

Universal detachment

Above all things, we must be disengaged even from the smallest objects of attachment. A divided heart can never be at peace. The jealousy of God which pursues in order to purify will trouble it incessantly with severe reproaches, or by afflicting silence. In vain will it endeavor to persuade itself that it is only through delicacy of conscience, and too great a refinement of piety that it torments itself about trifles which other people of solid piety have no care about. Notwithstanding all these efforts to calm itself, it feels that there is between it and God a wall of separation which is an effect of its resistance to His interior voice, and His designs upon it, until it will say from the depth of his heart with [Samuel] the young Prophet of Shiloh, *"Speak Lord, your servant hearkens," and is ready to obey without reserve,* God will in His mercy continually interrupt its repose.

Those pious persons to whom the soul communicates its troubles, even the ministers of God to whom it confides its conduct, will in vain exhort it to quiet the alarms of a timid conscience, abandon the impressions of imagination and sleep in peace. Their efforts are vain against the Lord who troubles it without ceasing and wills it to awake, and if the sweet accents of His voice will not suffice to move this rebellious heart, He will use against it the force of His arm, and overthrow it in as striking and humiliating a maneuver as he overthrew Saul in order to compel it to say as he said: *"Lord, what will you have me to do "* until without reasoning against the interior voice which would persuade it to a total renunciation of all things, it yields to its impression as the newly converted apostle did when struck with blindness. God is stronger than we are, and it is impossible that we should be at peace while we resist *Him.* "He is strong and powerful. Who shall resist Him and remain in peace?" (Job 9:4).

CHAPTER XIV

Conclusion of these three parts

1.

Here are many means, necessary means to acquire peace, and to preserve it. Perhaps they appear difficult to practice. How willingly would I soften their severity in favor of those weak souls who think the purchase of this great good too high a price [to pay]! "What?" say they, "observe oneself closely on every occasion and in every action — to act always by the inspirations of Divine grace and never by that of nature; to repress every passion, even the most lawful; to possess the equanimity of soul in the midst of the most trying revolutions; to pass suddenly from the most indulgent prosperity to the most afflicting adversity without suffering the least derangement of the interior?" If interior peace depends on so high a perfection, who can hope to possess it in this life?

It is true, we cannot hope to possess in this world a tranquility so perfect that it will never suffer the smallest alteration. But this virtue, like all others, has its different degrees. As here below, no one virtue can be acquired in its whole extent since we are in a state of progression, must we therefore neglect the practice of them? Timid souls, this is an exaggeration of the perfection of virtue to cover the shame of your negligence. It is your idleness which stops your progress; it is the *enemy* who seduces you. He concealed from you at first the beauty of virtue to prevent the effect of her attractions; he now displays its perfections by exaggerations which terrify you.

Scarcely do you make a step in the thorny ways of holiness, but he entices you to aim at a summit in order to discourage you in the outset. But you may disappoint his malicious artifices by a firm and tranquil resolution, supported by confidence in God, who awaits you on the holy mountain, not only to meet and receive you, but also to reach you His hand, and help you to ascend it. Sigh, indeed, and weep that you yet remain at the foot, but do not be content with barren tears, instead of filling your heart with generous resolutions of climbing to the top. *He* who bids you advance from virtue to virtue, and who even commands you to desire it, will fill you with the strength of His abundant benedictions. Begin with His assisting hand, and new strength and courage will flow from your feeblest endeavors.

Repress, at least, the most violent of your passions which are as contrary to the health of your body, as to that of your soul. Endeavor to do some good without too much eagerness; this will be difficult at first, but by desiring to practice what is so, you will insensibly obtain what you always desire. Nourish this desire by frequent reflections on the advantages of that peace of which the demon endeavors to deprive you, and on the facility with which you may surmount the obstacles he throws in your way, and exaggerates to deter you from persevering.

2.

Of the advantages of this peace, I have already spoken, but it is very certain all has not been said, nor can be said. This peace frees us from the tyranny of the demon whose empire is in the dwelling of disorder, confusion, and trouble. It drives him out of our heart, shuts up its avenues, and makes our soul firm and unshaken against his attacks. This peace is the reign of God within us which we petition for every day, and ought to desire above all things. It is the joy of this life, and a powerful means to procure us the felicity of the next. It is as a pledge and foretaste of the eternal rest of the saints. This peace is the distillation of Christian perfection; the knot which binds all virtues together, and without which none can be truly acquired. In the possession of this virtue, all others are possessed, as it is the center of all; or rather charity is the point to which they all tend, and peace is the guide which conducts them to her.

This peace is all divine; divine in its principle. God alone forming it in us, and with us, divine in its effects, uniting us to Him, who makes His dwelling in peace, divine in its recompense which is the God of peace Himself; divine in its model, since the peaceable are numbered among the children of God, and are known to be such by this mark; divine through Him who offers it to us, and by the price through which He has purchased it for us. A man-God has merited it for us with His blood (St. Francis de Sales, Ep. 26, L. 4).

3.

As to the facility of acquiring it, it must not be judged as we judge of human things which are difficult to acquire in proportion as they are precious and valuable, unless we esteem it the more for its rareness, and the price it has cost. Although in this world, it has neither its price nor its recompense, and we may apply to it all that

Solomon says of the merit of wisdom of which peace is the perfection.

Yet, everyone may possess it if they will labor for it; nor can they be deprived of it but by their negligence. We are not told to go and seek it in heaven, or to descend in the depths, or pass over the seas to find it. It is contained within ourselves; within our own soul. There it has been found by those against whom the world and hell itself conspired in order to deprive them of even the hope of it, and who certainly never would have enjoyed it had they not sought it in the enclosure of this interior solitude where neither man nor demons could penetrate.

There it has been found by those who would have sought it in vain in the most remote deserts, because they sought exteriorly and at a distance what they possessed close by and within themselves, as a distracted person seeks on all sides for what they hold in their own hands without perceiving it. There it has been found by those who have uselessly labored to obtain it by austerities and other exterior exercises, but have found it seated and waiting for them at the door of their heart, as soon as they seriously determined to enter into it.

There even the profane philosophers have found it though it had entered only by the dim light of reason obscured by sin and irreligion, and having only discovered it superficially without gaining to the foundation, having also preserved the seeds of inquietude and trouble incited incessantly by the hidden folds of vanity in their heart. You who profess piety will be less ardent in the pursuit of this peace than even the pagans; will you be so blind, or so indolent as to neglect so great a good!

It is a treasure hidden, indeed, but hidden in your own soul by a multitude of distractions and follies which you can dissipate when you please. That requires much care and attention as does every good we aim at. Business diversions and crime itself, do they require none? Do they not engage us in more painful labors than the utmost we could undergo to acquire the most perfect peace? What is there in the order of salvation which does not cost?

Is holiness and eternal glory to be obtained for nothing? The cross we must bear, the struggles we must endure, the combat to be sustained, and that through our whole life. Are these but big words without meaning? If really you will not labor to acquire virtues, why do you deceive the world by putting on the appearance of them? Why deceive yourself by believing you desire them, and perhaps, even that you practice them because you read books which treat of them?

If really you wish to acquire virtues, you should be persuaded that both care and diligence are necessary. But if you will take the way of peace, you will obtain them sooner, and have less to suffer. Do not consider them in their whole extent; the obstacles in the way and means of attaining will both become familiarized by practice. The obstacles will not always occur, and the means will daily seem easier. A soul once established in peace is like a machine which goes of itself when once it is set in motion. It requires only the eye of the workman, as it were, to preserve it in its regularity of motion.

* * * * *

Thus far we have spoken of the theory of this peace of the soul. We will now speak of the practice in order to direct the way to it more particularly.

Part IV

ON THE PRACTICAL
ASPECTS OF THIS PEACE

= we must not then repress all sensible and lively motions of the interior — there are some to which we should yield ourselves without reserve. many marks are to be given by which they may be discerned, but it sufficient now to observe that they are to be connected with tranquillity in God, who is the author of them, and who having formed us in his image, desires us to imitate him in our conduct, and resemble him as far as our weakness permitts in a continual Activity, and a perfect Repose. ⸻

Chapter 7th (Suffer without inquietude the aridities of the soul.)

Far from seeking to excite a sensible enjoyment in our pious affections we must patiently suffer aridities, disgusts, and always give the preference to solid peace rather than to passing consolations arising either from natural feeling, or reluctantly granted to our excessive weakness. in truth it is commonly only weak Souls, little versed in interior life who seek for consolations with ardour, and afflict themselves in aridity. As soon as God ceases to caress them as a tender Mother caresses her little child at the breast, they think they are abandoned by him, and are tempted in their turn to Abandon him — generally they neglect his service, and always lose their peace of heart. this evil is so common that the most common spiritual books fully treat of it and from them I will draw only what is necessary to my Subject.
In the first place I acknowledge that it is sorrowful indeed to fulfil the most sacred duty of piety with a cold heart, dissipated mind, and returning to them always without zeal, obliged as it were to drag the heart by force remaining before God without feeling, in stupid indifference — praying

CHAPTER I

This peace is not to be sought with too much ardor.

1.

By now, you are seriously resolved to labor in earnest for interior peace, and practice every means proposed to you for acquiring it. You really desire to possess yourself, to possess Jesus, the King of Peace, whose empire is the empire of peace and who is so averse to trouble that He goes out from those souls who yield themselves to it, and will make use of that trouble as one of the most dreadful scourges of His vengeance to punish their infidelity. You desire to be devout and tranquil that Jesus may dwell with you — but this desire must be discreet; this peace must be pursued with care, not with anxieties. It is a work of patience rather than of effort, and the more effort you make to acquire this holy repose, the more distant you will be from it.

It is not by agitation that we obtain tranquility. Nor is it by exhortation that a sick man is made to sleep, or by detailed reasonings to prove to him its necessity, or by loud cries against those who disturb him, but by proper remedies to produce sleepiness, and by preserving quiet and silence around him. He himself will banish the tranquility if he tries too much to attract it, since it is by banishing reflection, care, and inquietude, we attract repose rather than by being occupied with the means of attaining it.

2.

You must enter into your own interior, if you desire to find peace which is in the very center of your soul. If at first you do not meet with it, it is because you do not penetrate within the temple, and instead of entering the tabernacle, where only the light of the Lord is to be seen, and the odor of His sweetness enjoyed; instead of reaching the sanctuary where an eternal silence reigns, you re-

93

main at the porch where the crowd presses on you, and the contention of passions are continually heard.

Perhaps, you are yet ignorant even that there is a place within you so sacred and remote as to be inaccessible to them — this superior part of your soul where faith and reason hold their empire and with them every Virtue. Withdraw yourself into this interior asylum and shut the door after you until tranquility returns.

3.

Suffer patiently what you cannot prevent. You will obtain merit even by suffering for your own faults. That interior disorder which the revolt of our passions causes is a consequence of sin and the disorder it has produced in our nature, but it is also its remedy, because it excites our vigilance, exercises our patience and humbles our pride.

The Son of God in clothing Himself with our flesh without taking its sins, has made the remedy to proceed from the cause. Pray to Him, indeed, to deliver you from the corruption with which you are infected, to extinguish the fire which devours you, to stop the commotions of the intestinal war which agitates you; for we must not look with indifference on those emotions which excite us to sin, or move us to be troubled. This would be either a secret approval or a careless negligence.

These revolts are never of any use, except when they excite us to courage. God never beholds them with complaisance, but only when they produce the triumphs of His love. Call Him to your help, since He alone can appease the tempest, but if yet, He appears to be sleeping while you are in agitation, lose not your courage or patience. It is enough that Jesus is with you.

The thought of your harassed mind, the phantoms of your heated imagination, the inquietude of your troubled heart, will come and go with precipitation, crowding on each other, and bounding round you on every side like a swarm of bees, but as Saint Francis de Sales assures you, they will do you no harm, if you will remain motionless in the midst of their commotion.

4.

When even the noise is so great, that you cannot hear yourself, still you must not be troubled; instead of regaining what you have lost, trouble will only deprive you of what you still possess. Actual peace consists in holding to nothing, not even to sensible peace itself. Whilst we still hold to a sensible peace, the most we will obtain will be some few fruits which are quickly exhausted, and never the seeds and root which are found only in a will entirely free.

Like worldly peace which consists in the enjoyment of goods which the enjoyer has not in himself, and which consequently cannot be of long duration, very different from that peace left to us by Jesus Christ which proceeds from the Holy Spirit dwelling in us, and is formed within us by a total and universal detachment, and by an entire disappropriation of even His sensible gifts. Also remark that Christ Jesus in leaving peace to us as a rich inheritance tells us that He gives it in a manner quite different from that which the world gives its peace. In truth, the world gives her peace exhorting us to enjoy what she presents, and attaches us to it, whilst Jesus in giving His detaches us from all, even from His sensible gifts.

5.

Assure yourself, as far as you are able, of your good will and resolution to serve God. Attach yourself entirely to His love. Detest with your whole heart whatever you may find in yourself contrary to it; desire to possess interior repose, and the holy joy which accompanies it in order to adore and bless in full liberty that God who is infinitely worthy of all adoration and praise. But if He permits you to remain in trouble, be not afraid.

Beware of believing as often even most pious souls have believed that God is greatly irritated against you, since He permits you to be beaten by so furious a tempest, and its floods to reach even your soul. Consider rather that He means by this trial to prove the strength of your good will for Him, and how much you will bear for His sake. Far from waiting (as too many have done) for the return of peace before you pour out your soul to His divine majesty it is your very trouble which should inspire you with the fullest and most consoling confidence.

God is never so near you as when you are suffering for Him, not only by pains from without, but by trouble from within. Say then to Him with tranquil simplicity: *"Lord, you see my condition. My soul is sorrowful and cast down; my mind is continually wandering; my imagination carrying me away, agitating and fatiguing me when I endeavor to stop it. The trouble of my heart is extreme; the gloomy clouds its fermentation creates, confuse and bewilder me. Scarcely do I know where I am; pain, grief, and fear, with wearisome reflections beset and overpower me, and hide from my sight whatever might comfort or console me. If it is your will to restore me to tranquility, one word of yours suffices to calm this troubled sea. One ray of your light can instantly dissipate the darkness of my soul and restore its serenity. If it is not your will, I submit without reply; I will wait your own time in silent humility. Your divine help is my security and consolation; nor do I doubt you will bestow it since your own mercy begs it for me."*

Were you even troubled to such excess as to be unable to make this prayer, nor scarcely any other? Yet be not disconcerted, but humbly say with your agonizing Savior, *"Thy will be done,"* Fiat voluntas tuas, and know that you will be more agreeable to God in this state of agitation and trouble than in that of the most devout tranquility.

CHAPTER II

Sensible devotion must not be sought too earnestly.

1.

We must act with regard to sensible devotion and fervor in the same manner as we do with regard to peace. Desire it without impatience, ask for it without inquietude, possess it without attachment, lose it without alarm; not considering it with indifference, since it is a restraint upon our passions, an assistance to our weakness, and a seasoning to our spiritual food. Lose not courage when it is taken away, since the grace of God is our invisible support, and the accomplishment of His will our nourishment. He alone will supply the place with all things to those who hold to Him alone.

Carefully preserve the fervor of interior and solid resolutions, without being anxious about the veritable fervor of sentiment. Cultivate it when it is given without thinking much about it; do without it when it is taken away without regretting it too much; lose it not through your own fault because it is a real good; nor be afflicted when it fails whatever may be the cause, because this would be a real evil.

Desire the milk of devotion like young children who know that it is good for them; but desire it also as reasonable children who know how to let go of it. An attachment to it will not a little retard our progress to the great work of our perfection and peace.

We may and we ought to enjoy the presence of Jesus as long as He will remain with us. Follow Him wherever He goes as the Apostles did; follow him step by step every moment; run to Him over the very waves of the sea like St. Peter; rest ourselves on His bosom like St. John. And yet, if He withdraws, bear His absence without sadness or chagrin because He certainly does it but for our good. "It is expedient I should go from you" (Jn 16:2, 6-7).

2.

If the absence of our Lord was necessary for the apostles and is still necessary for us, and if His visible presence could have been an obstacle to the perfection of the saints, what sensible good can there be, even spiritual, from which we ought not to detach ourselves entirely? To wish absolutely to follow Jesus in His absence, to endeavor to quit the earth and take a flight to heaven, is a reversal of His established order — disturbing the order of His Providence, and a useless unavailing fatigue. Wait in peace till clothed with strength from on high.

Wanting to be always at His right hand or His left is to know not what we ask; desiring to fix ourselves with Him on Tabor is indiscreet, and often proceeding from a spiritual sensuality or, what is worse, a secret vanity which is still more despicable, more disagreeable to God, and injurious to ourselves filling us with the desire of shining and being distinguished by fervor and enthusiasm in piety, like a body adorned by the luster of ornaments and graces. But what avails this subtle and deplorable ambition but to render us bombastic in devotion, as the vain and foolish are in their discourse and manners; as insupportable to the eyes of God, as the vain and affected are in the eyes of rational and sensible men.

Conduct yourself before God with great humility and simplicity, not with fervor and impatience. You desire to take your flight to heaven, to rise above the stars forgetting that one humble prayer will carry you further than your presumptuous flight. Wearied with endeavors, foolish with elevation, you fall, and are bruised in the descent. Desiring to fly too high disables you from walking with even an ordinary step, and often you are obliged to drag yourself through shameful disorders, the very filth of the earth, which is generally the consequence of vain fervor and devotion badly regulated. The pains occasioned by the excesses of this fervor are too acute, the illusions which result from it too frequent, and interior peace too much affected by them to allow us to drop the subject here. Let us examine it more particularly.

* * * * *

*On not making too many efforts to obtain fervor
when preparing for confession*

1.

When you are on the point of presenting yourself at the tribunal of Penance, you are in great pain to excite contrition. You multiply reflections, representing to your mind the most awful and vivid ideas of the majesty of God, or the rigor of His judgments and severity of His vengeance, and perhaps, of the greatness of His benefits and the magnificence of His glory, the eternity of His recompense. But your mind becomes exhausted by these reflections so multiplied, and your heart contracted by its efforts to express its affections.

Alarmed by this disposition, you redouble the efforts which occasion it, add reflection to reflection, and effort to effort, to excite what you imagine to be devotion. The evil does but increase because its sources are multiplied; weakness and discouragement follow, and from desiring to approach the tribunal with a sensible contrition, you bring only a gloomy sadness, and a sort of despair. Your zeal is edifying, but your situation pitiable. Yet the remedy will be found in a simple explanation.

2.

What is contrition, or attrition, which occasions you so much pain? *"It is,"* you will reply, *"a sincere sorrow for having offended God, either because we have really offended, or because we have lost Him."* But I would ask, *"Is it a pain in the head, or of some other part of the body?"* *"No,"* you answer, *"It is a pain in the heart."* But as too much light can never be thrown on matters of piety, let me again ask, *"Is it in this heart of flesh, which is the center of your corporal life?"* *"No, it is a regret of the soul which arises from a detestation of sin, and sorrow for*

having committed it." "Why, then, will you torment your body to excite
what proceeds only from the soul, and can only be produced from it with
the help of divine grace? Why fatigue your sight by fixed regard or
contemplation of troubling objects: your head, by strong application, and
your whole body by painful positions?" Even these reflections of the
mind most proper to excite the sentiments of the heart, ought not
to be too multiplied or extended. They would become a fatigue
instead of an assistance.

The soul exhausted by the contention would feel itself unable to rise towards God. A simple thought, a tranquil affection,
a consoling resolution, one look at that goodness which always
rejoices the heart which loves, will easily produce in you the effect
you desire and seek for in vain, by efforts which diminish devotion and are injurious both to the health of your soul and body.

                                   3.

In addition, is it not true that you live distanced from sin and the
occasions of it? That you detest not only that which gives death to
the soul, but also that which weakens it? That when you have
fallen in it, you were sorry for it, and took precautions for the
future? Is it not true that without waiting the occasion of the
Sacrament, you often are grieved for your past sins, and daily
faults? If so, you have what you seek for, or rather what you seek
for is far inferior to what you really possess, since you have as far
as we can judge a true contrition, and what you seek is but an
illusive shadow of it.

Your disposition is uniformly to prefer God to all the goods
of the world, to detest sin as the greatest of all evils, and mortal sin
above all. This is all that is required for true contrition. Let this
disposition be put in action to obtain the matter of the Sacrament,
and it is sufficient. With it, you have the necessary preparation to
receive the sacrament with fruit before you have excited it. By
exciting it, you only lose a part of your preparation by exhausting
your heart and disturbing its peace.

ARTICLE TWO

*Too great a desire of fervor in communion
must be avoided.*

1.

You intend to approach the holy table. Be careful not to dishonor it by affected manners, and ridiculous gestures which are almost inseparable from the efforts which attract a sensible devotion. Be serious, grave, simple, modest, without singularity, and without precipitation.

Be interiorly to the eyes of God what you appear externally to the eyes of men. Approach Him in a modest peaceful manner, adore His Majesty, admire His goodness, acknowledge your nothingness in His sight, lay before Him your miseries and beg to be united to Him offering your heart to Him with as much tranquility as you could perform any ordinary exercise of religion. By forcing yourself, you may perhaps obtain a sensible fervor, but it will only deceive you, since when it fails (and nothing forced can be lasting) the constraint of the interior will prevent the divine grace from penetrating the soul, and often dissipate that which it possessed before.

You will not know how to approach God without those pious sensations and enjoyments which drew you to Him. Besides, your aridity will throw you into extreme alarms on the state of your conscience. You will fear that some secret sin has deprived you of that fervor you had relied on and of the unction which had filled you with delight. Either you will resolve to deprive yourself of the sacrament, or you will receive it in such sorrowful perplexity that you will lose almost all the fruit of it.

2.

There are persons who after having a long time frequented the sacraments with success deprive themselves entirely of them because they no longer experience this fervor. Relying too much on sensible devotion which can never suffice for the immortal edifice, and having built upon this earthly clay, the moment it fails, their work falls in ruin and they themselves are buried in it to the scandal of their brethren and loss of their own souls. For many years together, they are separated from the holy table, living without remorse in a sort of excommunication pronounced at the tribunal of their own errors. And what is still more deplorable, this life so little edifying is finished by very doubtful death.

Others again, who in the first beginnings of their piety, never participate in the divine sacrament except with a heart full of trouble, and view with a sort of terror the approach of those periods which brought them to the holy table. This disposition alarms them, and through a very common error, they seek the cause in their confessions with which they are never satisfied. They torture themselves to obtain tranquility, and as the Sacrament of Penance must immediately precede that of the Eucharist, one subject of torment succeeds another, and each becomes continually more painful, and consequently a greater burden.

In this deplorable state, they drag out days of sorrow, exhausting their strength, and living a dying life; a sad example of the sufferings those are exposed to, and the risk they run in the path of virtue, who go on without experience and without guide, without confidence and without docility. But as soon as the heart is opened, and the wound is searched, the source of their pain is made known to them which was occasioned solely by their desire to feel that which they ought only to love, and thus endeavoring to lift the veil of Faith, though it is held down by an all powerful hand.

Light restores them to peace. They begin to await from the hand of God what they had imagined their own exertions could procure. A tranquil diligence is substituted to their eager inquietude. The heart more peaceful and susceptible of the influence of divine grace, which interior trouble and alarms had interrupted, feels the power of the divine benediction. God is moved by their docility, to give them that sense of the presence of Jesus when they least expect it, which they had so much desired. What before had been their torment from mistaken piety, becomes now the sweet consolation of their life.

3.

It is to be understood that here I speak of those active devotees to whom moderation appears coldness. "What!" say they, "approach God without feeling, do the greatest and most holy of all actions like a common exercise? Take no care to put one's self in the dispositions the Church orders us to bring and which the holiness of the sacrament itself exacts of us? Not to prove oneself as the apostle directs, [or approve of all that one is, however dry he/she may be]; unite oneself to our Savior with a tranquil air resembling indifference and contempt?"

No, I would not have you approach this God who is all love with coldness, but is it with your own fire or with His you ought to burn? Certainly, yours will quickly disappear before the ardor of this consuming fire. I fear not to tell you, and you ought not to fear to think that this great action should be done with the same tranquility as the rest of your pious exercises, but with very different care.

I would not have you negligent of the necessary dispositions to nourish yourself with the Bread of Heaven, but would earnestly desire you to count the peace of your heart among the principal ones. It is the only one you do not endeavor to acquire, and seem rather to take every measure to destroy.

You wish to prove yourself? Far from dissuading you from it, I exhort you to do it; nor can you exceed in your endeavor as long as it only contributes to augment your humility, the love of God, confidence in Him, desire to receive Him — not troubles,

alarms, and separation from the sovereign remedy for all evils. I
am far from approving the dryness of your heart. On the contrary,
I advise you not to augment it by the heat of your desires and
vivacity of your movements. Wretched is that tranquility which
proceeds from indifference for God, but wretched also is that
eagerness which arises from excess of self-love.

The tranquility produced by a medium between both is a just
proportion. Prepare yourself then in the best manner you are able
for this great action without relying too much on your own care.
Animate your zeal without losing your repose; exert yourself
gently; moderate your ardor, possess yourself courageously and
without indolence. This is all that God requires of you.

4.

To agitate one's self and lose the peace of our soul — can this be
a good preparation for a sacrament whose great end is to preserve
us in peace? To destroy the effect in order to practice the means?
What a reversal of order! This puts it out of our power to possess
that peace which is the fruit of a good Communion, and exposes
us to make a bad one, although we exhaust ourselves even to the
loss of our peace to make it well.

Our ardent desire for sentiments of devotion when we are to
communicate, the eager care we take to excite them, our inquietude when we do not succeed serve (says the author of the
Imitation of Christ) but to render us less disposed for the communion we desire excessively to prepare for; to interrupt the effusions
of that grace we so inordinately desire to possess, and to destroy
in us all devotion instead of increasing it.

The Sacrament of the Eucharist is without doubt a powerful
means of salvation and sanctification, since in itself it contains the
source of every grace. Yet, I dare to assert that if you cannot be fed
with this life-giving food without considerably disturbing that
peace of which it is the life itself, it would be better that you should
seldom approach and possess it undisturbed, than suffer it to be

frequently disturbed by repeating your Communions. I know of many saints who communicated but seldom; but I know of none who did not possess peace of soul. How could they have been saints without it, without that deep solid and intimate peace which is holiness itself, as we have already declared with Saint Augustine.

5.

In truth, there is a great fund of self-love hidden under this veil of devotion. We are quite troubled at having so little fervor, because we had the presumption to believe we could attain it by our own strength. We persuade ourselves that there can be no means of obtaining fervor displeasing to God. We have not the humility to acknowledge ingenuously, those faults which have destroyed or weakened in us this happy disposition, or that confidence in Him which alone can restore it to us. A little reflection would convince us that this internal agitation and commotion cannot produce the fire of divine love, but only that of imagination and natural activity. Yet, we wish to be fervent by all means because we desire to be contented with ourselves without much examination whether it is the means also of contenting God.

These communicants whose zeal is so animated may be compared to certain persons of the world who have the same disposition arising from the same principle of precipitancy. They desire always to be found in the most exact order, and that you should know that they are so. Should they be unexpectedly visited while in a time of derangement and disorder, they are immediately in motion, crying out to their servants, and bewildering everybody, perplexing both themselves and their visitors who are secretly grieved and received very badly from an excessive desire to do it well. If a friend should welcome you in this manner, would you not be grieved? Would you not be more desirous of his presence than of seeing the exactness and order of his house? Would you not perhaps take the freedom of saying to him, *"It is*

for yourself I am come not for your servants or furniture. For pity's sake
stay with me, and let me quietly enjoy the pleasure of your company
which is all I desire."

Our Lord would tell you much the same, so much He desires
to familiarize Himself to us: His delight is to be with the children
of men (Pr 8), and especially with the poor, when they carry with
them that humility which is the first badge of their state. It is with
the lame, the blind and paralytic He fills His feast chamber (Lk 14).
He calls the little ones, and those whose approach to Him would
seem a presumption and folly (Pr 3) if He did not see in the first a
sincere determination to renounce the childishness of infancy,
and in the second the desire of true wisdom (Pr 4:6). It is yourself
He asks and not your gifts. He loves purity of heart, separation
from the world, the silence of the passions, and great tranquility
of soul. Sublime thoughts are less pleasing to Him than a humble
acknowledgment of our miseries, for these make known the
greatness of His mercies in the sacrament of His love. In vain, will
you expect to prepare yourself by your own efforts. The love
which invites you can alone supply your indigence which confounds you. He tells you, *"Come receive me, and let it suffice that I*
myself command it."

6.

Consider the interior disposition of the saints when they have
received the Savior in the sacrament of His body, and their
exterior deportment when they were so happy as to receive Him
in their house, or approach Him during His mortal life. Zacchaeus,
when he least expected it, received Him in his house, and with as
much respect as affection, looking on Him with simplicity and
candor. Taken by surprise he treated Him as well as he could
without disturbing his own joy nor that of his guests by his hurry
or inquietude.

St. Peter also received the Savior in his poor dwelling without troubling himself about what was wanting to its decency, well

persuaded that since nothing could be hidden from Him, and still He would come to lodge in so poor a place, He surely would be satisfied with what He would find there. Far from being disturbed, or imagining Jesus would be offended by the poverty of his reception, St. Peter freely asked a favor of Him. He presented Him his sick mother, and begged Him to heal her.

The two sisters of the Gospel are favored in their turn with a visit from their divine master. Martha was impatient to receive Him well, and was reproved for it; Mary received Him with more humility than care, with more repose than ardor; the soul at rest as well as the body, *sedens*. She listened to the words of life which fell from His lips, and listened in silence, *audiabat*; she was highly praised. The Son of God goes to the house of the centurion. He goes in haste because they pressed Him. The centurion advances to meet Him saying, "Lord, I am not worthy that you should come under my roof. Why should you take the unnecessary trouble. At this moment, in the place we are standing, speak only the word, command the sickness of my servant, as I myself command my soldiers and servants, and it will depart in any instant."

The Savior presented Himself to St. John to be baptized. "I, Lord, I baptize you?" replied St. John. "I myself should be too happy to receive that favor from you, instead of exercising it on your divine person." Jesus insists; John obeys. He sees with astonishment his God at his feet, but without being troubled; he was wholly occupied with the fulfillment of His blessed will. After acknowledging to Him his insufficiency, he baptized Him with a heart filled with love and respect. His mind was tranquil, and his exterior composed.

The greatest of all examples was that of the Blessed Virgin at the moment she was exalted to the highest dignity God could grant to a pure creature, that of *Mother of God*. True, she was at first a little troubled but it was because she heard great praises bestowed on her which she thought were unmerited. As soon as the angel ceased speaking about her, and announced the divine mystery to be fulfilled in her, not only did she acquiesce to what he declared, *ecce ancilla Domini* (Behold the handmaid of the Lord), but she also desired that it be accomplished in her. She testified to this with simplicity, though, filled with the sublimity of the mystery and her own nothingness (*Fiat mihi*).

Do you recognize in any of these examples your own forced tremblings and exhausting agitations — this fire taken from your own oven, not from the Altar; from your natural temper, not from the Lord? You see nothing but humility, candor, simple expressions, and ingenuous sentiments; and could you see the interior of these great models, you would see nothing but tranquil motions flowing from their heart, as from their source, proportioned to their degrees of grace, and the actual impression of the Holy Spirit.

Imitate their conduct, without adding your pretended fervor. Open your heart with simplicity to Jesus as Zacchaeus opened his house: Acknowledge to Him your unworthiness as the centurion did; beg Him to heal your soul, as St. Peter begged the cure of his Mother. Alone with Him, alone in the depth of your heart, listen to Him, like Magdalene, to the words He will speak to it in this solitude. Show him your sincere disposition to obey His will like St. John, desire to be intimately united to Him like Mary, and to render this union perfect beg Him to come often to you.

Commune then, without too much anxiety to possess this sensible fervor and vivacity of sentiment which depends not on yourself, and which God does not value in you as much as humility, candor, tranquility, confidence and the care of your advancement in virtue. This you seem to consider but little. Commune often, and many times a week, on the advice of a pious, enlightened and prudent director.

If your attraction to this adorable sacrament is accompanied with a sense of your unworthiness and you join to it the practice of good works: flight from the world, a life of recollection and mortification long tried, separation from all sin even venial, (I say separation, not exemption, which is incompatible with human frailty) a sincere desire of advancing in virtue, watchfulness over yourself as far as your situation permits. Commune, I say, although you appear to present nothing to Jesus but a dry heart and a mind enveloped in darkness. Remember, darkness praises God as well as light, and we may present ourselves with confidence in His sanctuary in this state of aridity on which He delights to display the luster of His glory.

CHAPTER III

We are not to be troubled by our distastes and fickleness.

1.

After all that has been said on aridities and distaste, when we were considering the means of acquiring peace, it remains now to apply our observations. However little taste we may have for holy exercises, yet persevere in them constantly and preserve your peace by steadiness of behavior. Should your prayer become an insipid and even a troublesome employment, bear it patiently, and join to the sacrifice of the lips that of the deprivation of sensible enjoyments. Carefully banish from your mind that too common error of imagining that God no longer accepts the sacrifice of praise when our heart is shut up, since on the contrary, it is when it is most afflicted He desires the offering of it, by which we draw down His grace, light and joy.

Be strengthened then by the persuasion that the greater your difficulty is in praying, the more agreeable your prayer is to God, and the more profitable to yourself, provided your own negligence does not occasion it. Unite it to the prayer of your agonized Savior which was not less meritorious for being accompanied with a mortal sadness, and by the example of this Divine Master. Even prolong it sometimes, the better to conquer the enemy, or self-love which would oblige you to abandon or shorten it.

2.

Has prayer become not only painful and wearisome, a burden on your heart, a void and wandering of your mind rather than an application of it; a scene for the idle dreams of your imagination? Humble yourself before God, and recollect that your sins fully deserve this coldness from Him, and that yours in His presence are the effects of your infidelities to Him, or of His wise designs on you. If He does not permit you to sit down with His children and nourish yourself with the delicious food He gives to them, beg Him at least to bestow on you the crumbs which fall from His table. Contemplate their happiness and wish to partake of it, but without inquietude; apply yourself without fatigue, and if you cannot gain the height of the mountains like the hart, hide yourself in the holes of the rocks like the hares.

Wrap yourself in your own nothingness, and far from affecting a forced useless and dangerous elevation, keep yourself seated in your own darkness, and beg Him to enlighten you. Say to Him from the bottom of your tranquil heart: *"Lord, behold me, in your presence without reflection, without sentiment like a stupid animal. Yet, I will persevere in prayer, and if I cannot do much for You, at least I will remain before You. I will glorify You by my sufferings, if I cannot by my fervor. I detest from my heart the sins and negligences which separate me from You, but I willingly receive the pain, and even were I not guilty, I would wish to be submissive.*

"Your Will, always adorable, is precious to me in its very rigors. I adore You, your sovereignty though I cannot taste your sweetness. Though You should strike me with a final blow, my last sigh should be an act of confidence. Should I become like that abandoned vine which You forbid even the dews of heaven to visit, and leave to a frightful solitude, I will yet hope for your return, and that from the height of heaven, You will cast a look of pity in the vine your right hand has planted, and visit it with the influence of your love; that time will yet come when the barren desert shall change to a fertile scene in which You will delight to shed the luster of your glory and the radiance of your beauty. You delight, dear

Lord, to work upon nothing; *behold me, and if I am yet something in my own eyes, hasten my annihilation that You may begin your work."*

3.

Conduct yourself in the same manner in your Communions, your practices of mortification, your services to your neighbor, and in general, in whatever relates to piety on the maxim already established that the more pain and violence you experience in these practices the more crowns you will gain, and the more certain you will be of drawing the divine favor upon you. The cross is your inheritance if you desire to be among the followers of Jesus. Build your spiritual edifice upon the living rock of Calvary where Jesus in the fullness of His age developed the profound mysteries of His doctrine, and consummated the work of your salvation, and not on the good things of Egypt where He lived feeble and unknown.

Is it to amuse yourself with some trifling enjoyments you have entered in the service of God, or to work the salvation of your soul through all sorts of labors? Woe to you, if after many years of a devout life, you are at your death but a child of an hundred years, and if after having sown during life in the sensuality of the flesh, and not in the spirit of solid virtue, you can only reap in the end humiliation and corruption.

Let not the sweetness enjoyed by others excite your impatience at your own dryness. They have like you their gloomy days. Their present delights are either a recompense from God for their labors, or a gratuitous effusion of His mercy; you should neither compare your own virtues with those they practice, nor be jealous of the favors with which they are rewarded.

4.

It is true, you will say, God does not bestow the same favors on everyone. He is the absolute Master of them and I am far from complaining of the distribution He makes of them. When He grants them it is always a favor, and when He withholds them He is never unjust. I know also that I grow more and more unworthy of them, and this afflicts me most. I should not be uneasy, if I was not unfaithful. If I run ever so much to obtain the crown, it is not in order to take it from another, but to obtain my own, which I am at every moment in danger of losing. Yesterday, I was fervent, today I am tepid, perhaps tomorrow I shall be quite cold.

But I tell you, you know not your own heart and its alternatives, the graces with which you are favored and the different manner of them — that you will perhaps be tomorrow what you were yesterday. Because you were fervent then, it does not follow you should be so now, and that it is through your own fault that you are not. It is much to be wished that what you call a coldness which confounds you, may not in your impatience turn to an outburst of emotion and create giddiness.

The life of our soul, like that of our body, is a mixture of day and night — light and darkness. While it is day, we must work courageously, and when it is night, suffer *patiently*; it is a great deal, if we do not dissipate then what we had before acquired; it would be quite as foolish to be surprised at the weakness we then feel, as at the shades of darkness when it is night. "Do not much rely on your present disposition which will soon change (says the author of the *Imitation of Christ*) while you live you will be, in spite of yourself, subject to changes and varieties: sometimes in joy, sometimes in sorrow; sometimes tranquil, sometimes troubled; sometimes devout, at other times without devotion; at one time fervent, at another careless; sometimes serious, sometimes light." But a prudent soul well versed in spirituality is above all these vicissitudes, and little attentive to what goes on within him, or which way the wind of inconsistency blows; it presses on to its aim, which is its advancement in virtue, and firm amidst every variety and change.

5.

St. Francis de Sales tells us not to be surprised at these vicissitudes, or alarmed at the weakness which succeeds the most courageous resolutions assuring us (Ep. 47, L. 4) that God will make of our miseries the treasure of His mercies, and of our weakness the throne of His power, if we support them with humility, gentleness, and tranquility; if we do not lose confidence in our weakness and obscurities; if we avoid impatience, haste and trouble, which will only, he says, "tangle the thread of your work, and embarrass you by multiplicity of thought and confusion of desires, like a bird entangled in a net." Assuredly, it will not be the way to advance in the path of virtue, or regain the fervor you have lost. Much time is required to disengage and restore yourself to the liberty you enjoyed before you yielded yourself to a turbulent impetuosity, and much more still will be lost by pursuing an artificial fervor, which the Demon profiting by our weakness, will not fail to present and cause you to withdraw from the truth.

These vicissitudes of which you complain were often experienced by Saint Francis de Sales. He endured them without alarming himself, or yielding to inquietude and impatience which he everywhere condemns. "Going out from my interest," he says in one of his letters, "I seemed to have come from the other world, and I scarcely knew how to speak any more of this one. A multitude of business affairs and their many distractions have insensibly relaxed this vivacity of sentiment; nothing remains for me of this retreat but a dry practice of the resolutions I have taken."

Imitate Him by your fidelity, by a conduct always serious and recollected, by a continual mortification of your passions and ardor, by patience in waiting long for the Lord who waited for you so long, who so often presented Himself to the door of your heart without ever attempting to break it; who beseeched you without troubling you; who offered Himself without impatience; and withdrew without anger, and still incessantly returned. This tranquil expectation of fervor joined to a reasonable care and sincere desire to obtain it, is the surest means of recalling it sooner, of possessing it constantly, and of becoming superior by our fidelity to the changes and varieties which depend not on us.

6.

Saint Teresa of Avila also was subject to these vicissitudes, sometimes with a courage nothing could shake; sometimes with a timidity which was alarmed by the least pain; sometimes with fervor which seemed to be unchangeable; sometimes with a languor which seemed impossible to animate; at times with a disengagement which raised her easily above everything; at others with affections of debasing attachments which lowered her, as it were, beneath everything. Yet the surprising changes she not only experienced in herself, but had also observed in other holy souls served only to show her the weakness of human nature without discouraging her, and the strength of grace without creating pride.

The more frequent these changes were, the more sensible she was of the effect of these two objects which, as it were, balanced each other, and kept her in a right medium between excessive fear, and too much confidence. Knowing that day and night succeeded each other she was neither frightened by one, or dazzled by the other.

If these great saints, and almost every servant of God has felt these weaknesses, darkness and aridities, should we be surprised if the strength, grace, and light with which we are sometimes favored should be interrupted? If they found no resource in their infirmities but humble prayer, ought we to seek it in presumptuous efforts? If they were persuaded that their nature, however active and upright it might be, could produce nothing but what is natural, and contented themselves to act with moderation according to the measure of present grace, can we believe that we can add anything of our own to strengthen our grace? Or would we interrupt its effects by our multiplied exertions, rather than renounce the vain satisfaction we seek in our sensible devotion?

If, with the prudent Virgins, the saints quietly awaited the return of the Bridegroom, contenting themselves to watch and keep their lamps in good order; should we be wise to go out without trimming our lamps, without oil, amidst the darkness and dangers of the night, to meet Him whose approach we ought to wait for; wait for Him then in peace, without impatience, and yet without falling asleep. If He delays His coming, redouble your vigilance, persuaded that His promise will not fail, and He will not long delay (Hab 2:3). Is there a contradiction in saying that *deferring is not delaying*? No, for they are the words of truth itself. It sometimes seems to impatient self-love or unenlightened zeal, perhaps also to our pious desires, that Our Lord is slow in coming, and His absence very long; but in truth, His coming is always without delay, because He comes always precisely at the very moment His infinite wisdom has marked, and our true needs require it.

CHAPTER IV

In order to preserve interior peace,
we should desire virtues themselves with moderation,
and practice them without too much ardor.

ARTICLE ONE

Moderation in the desires of virtue

1.

Perhaps, it might seem surprising when we say that we ought to be sober even in wisdom, if we did not repeat the very words of St. Paul who supports them with the whole authority of his apostleship. For although there can never be excess in virtue, yet there may be a great deal in the ideas we form of it, the desires we conceive, and the practices we follow, because virtue is found in surroundings one keeps away from, and much more difficult to find than the perfect equilibrium of the body. As a trembling and quick hand can never find balance, so those ardent desires which throw us in trouble and sorrow will never bring us to the virtue we propose. For they disturb the peace of the soul which is both the principle and fruit of every virtue.

Unexperienced beginners consider these vehement desires as gales of wind which drive them out of their way. St. Francis de Sales, who was so enlightened in the guidance of the interior, bids us keep our heart at liberty, and not to press it too hard by our too great desire of perfection (Ep. 59, L. 3).

As all virtues are linked with each other and give mutual support, no one of them can be opposed to the other. This principle is invariable, and from it we may judge of certain pious movements and particular attractions which are not to be considered as a production of virtue from the moment we find them in opposition to obedience and peace. The first of these virtues is a living rule, evident and easily applied. The second is interior and hidden, but may be easily discerned by an attentive soul.

We should only desire virtues for the glory of God and our sanctification. The glory of God consists in the accomplishment of His holy will, and our sanctification in renouncing our own. Now God wills that peace should hold her reign in our souls over all the virtues, regulating their desires and directing their practice. Should our will reverse this order, it would be a formal opposition to the will of God.

2.

There are two things in virtue which may excite our desire. One is virtue itself and the great good it procures us; the other is the beauty of virtue and the glory we will obtain by it. The saints who had only the first object in view sought perfection with tranquil desires, and peaceful exertions. We also aim at the second, and perhaps, in consequence of our corruption, even give it the first place. We desire so much to be perfect that we become impatient when we perceive we are not; nor should our separation from mankind (in which perhaps we are) deceive us or induce us to believe that vanity has no part in our desires, since we are never so entirely separated from the world, and pride is eager to fasten itself on everything; it bends itself so far as even to seek the applause of those it despises. Were we quite alone, we would still be sensible to this attraction, without reflecting that nothing is so destructive to virtue as our own complacency. The fall of the ancient anchorites who were lost by vanity is a strong and fearful example (Fathers of the Desert).

Let us accustom ourselves to look at our sins and imperfections incessantly. Consider seldomly and only when absolutely necessary, our progress in virtue and our exemption from certain defects. We must wish as far as charity permits that the eye of our neighbor should never stop but on the first object. Love to be despised, and most of all, let us despise ourselves; then our restless desires will soon cease, and we will not be in danger of letting our lamps go out, even if we should lose the oil of public esteem, or the good opinion of those we most value.

3.

You propose to yourself at first, the very perfection of virtue, and you consider it, not as a distant object towards which you are gradually to progress, but as a height you desire to reach by excessive efforts. Its gradations weary you, while another more prudent than yourself who makes use of them will arrive much sooner and without fatigue to the very point you have vainly desired to attain. The whole work of our sanctification is divided into difficult beginnings, insensible progress, and happy consummation in the order of grace as in that of nature.

God wills that the increases should be gradual and imperceptible, and you desire to join the two extremities and pass over the gradual process. The husbandman is more patient than you are, and you should make use of his examples since it is to him the Savior sends you for instruction. He first prepares the ground, then casts in the grain which he loses sight of without fearing to lose it, or his time, or labor. The wheat appears after his patience has been a little tried, but it will be much more tried before he gathers the increase. At first, it is a tender *shoot*, then an *herb*, then the *blade* in which the wheat is formed, and ripened by degrees imperceptibly to the laborer (Mk 4:26).

Jesus has sown over you the grain of His words and planted the seeds of virtue in your heart, and you are impatient to produce the fruits? You would hasten by the ardor of your actions what patience alone can bring to maturity? You will spoil all, and lose all from a desire to feast the eyes of your self-love with the fruits of your labor, and the wish to gather them before the time without either patience or discretion. You say and you also think that it is zeal for the glory of God, and your advancement. But in truth, it is an irregular self-love, want of confidence in God and distrust of the divine grace.

You expect too much from yourself, and it is on yourself alone you rely without perceiving it, instead of placing in the treasury of Providence whatever good you do and there abandoning it. You daily expect to perceive your progress and count your gain as a merchant does his percent as the day ends. Not satisfied with the hope of harvest, you wish to see it growing under your eyes, Oh, soul of little faith! At least confide in God who will receive your work in His own hands, as the laborer confides to the ground the seed which he sows in it.

God, who is too just to forget your good actions, will insensibly and without your knowledge advance you in virtues. Should He sometimes let you see their first shoots in order to encourage you, be careful how you expose these precious shoots to the rigor of the season, which not having yet any depth of root will be soon dried up by the scorching sun. The contradiction of the wicked, and the persecution that the world will not fail to raise against you, would stifle this hope of harvest in its birth.

You are weak; unhappy, if you do not feel it, and unhappier still, if feeling your weakness, you would imprudently expose it. But do not imagine that the progress you make would render you motionless in the midst of winds and storms. Perhaps, as you advance, you will find yourself still more and more agitated, and bent more violently towards the earth when you are most loaded with fruit. Those who are troubled and astonished to find in themselves earthly inclinations and, as says St. Francis de Sales, are not content that their plant is firm and well rooted, but are unwilling that a single leaf should be moved by the wind, are not sufficiently acquainted with the character of the human heart, the nature of virtue, nor the economy of grace.

* * * * *

Article Two

Moderation in the imitation of virtues...
We are not to attempt imitating all that we see done by others.

1.

To imagine we ought to imitate all the good we see others do is
an error, and a presumption which can only produce dangerous
distractions, useless efforts and a troubled heart. God does not
give equal strength to all in the practice of virtue, because all are
not called to the same degree of glory. He gives five talents to one,
while to another He gives but two. Will you ask Him why He has
many dwellings in His mansions, or why He does not give you the
first place? This would be a daring assumption of His rights by
pretending to raise yourself above the rank He has destined for
each one, without waiting for His will; while on the contrary,
sober wisdom waits all from Him and is content with the measure
of grace destined to it, confining its whole attention not to lose
what is bestowed, and all its fervor in asking every moment
according to the extent of this same grace.

Where are you running? Why are you so hurried? You have
seen an act of heroic virtue performed, and you cannot rest a
moment without imitating it? You perform it but fruitlessly, in the
precipitancy of your zeal. You have the will to do this action, but
had you the call? Did God require this service of you? At the time
you are performing this one, how many are others doing? Can you
be everywhere, and imitate them all? Oh! Stop. Remain in the
place where God has placed you, should it even be the lowest;
modestly wait until He bids you come higher. You will discern His
voice when He calls by the peace it will bring to your heart, while
an ambitious piety brings nothing but trouble.

Watch without inquietude in that moderate degree of virtue
proportioned to your strength and calling, yet always with the
desire of greater perfection. God will, perhaps, bring you to the

highest after strengthening you in humility, and making you for a long time feel the sense of your indigence.

The most certain means of obtaining His favors is to confide in His goodness, and restrain ourselves modestly in that boundary where He has placed us, without envy or negligence. He does not desire everyone to serve Him in the same manner, but some in one way, some in another, according to their different talents and the light and strength bestowed on them.

To wish to undertake everything without awaiting His indication, without the evidence of His will, but precisely because it is a good, and that others do it, is imitating the imprudent zeal of those Hebrews who wished to be the deliverers of their people, and conquerors of their enemies, as well as the Maccabees, but whose enterprise could not be blessed by God because they were not the men of His right hand nor of His choice, who had been destined by Him to govern the people, and not to gain the conquest of nations.

2.

Did the saints themselves always practice the good they remarked in others? Did St. Louis, King of France, imitate the actual poverty of St. Francis? Did the Fathers of the Desert engage themselves in apostolic labors? I know that each one of them united every virtue in his own person; but did they always practice each one in the same manner and to the same degree? Those who knew they were surpassed and excelled by others, did they yield to impatience, envy or sadness? Had they been susceptible of these impressions at the sight of the abundance of others, and of their own indigence, they never would have found repose, for they always had a high opinion of their neighbor and a very mean one of themselves. If you expect a sense of your perfection to restore you to peace, you must either renounce entirely the claim to your peace or Christian humility.

Our Lord Himself has said: "Come, learn of me, I am meek and humble of heart," and this is His fundamental maxim. In vain, through an ambition and presumption which thinks itself capable of all things, would you persist in building your spiritual edifice on any other foundation but that of humility, or think of cementing it with anything but meekness. The souls of the just are as so many flowers in the garden of the heavenly spouse. All are not equally beautiful, or fragrant, but this very variety is an admirable proof of the divine wisdom which formed them.

Holiness has many forms, like grace from which it is produced. Let us bear our own fruit, and produce it in its proper time, looking on that of others only to admire it.

"What shall I do, my Father," said a solitary to an experienced Father whom he consulted. "Since I am in this desert, I have never been able to make more than three hundred prayers a day, and I hear that a young maid in the village makes as many as seven hundred. Her example confounds and troubles me." "And I," replied the wise old man. "I make only one hundred, yet I have no remorse; if you have any, it is because you do not all that is in your power to do."

How useful an example does this furnish us with? A solitary suffers great pains of conscience because he says only three hundred prayers a day — what a condemnation of our slothfulness, our dissipation, and indifference for prayer! A poor girl makes seven hundred. What is not even weakness capable of when it is animated by a lively faith, great courage, and fervor! A man of consummate virtue does not do as much as a poor maid.

Perfection, then, is independent of multiplicity of practice. God gives not, then, the same strength to all, nor does He require from all the same services. Therefore, we may be perfect in our degree by fidelity to what God requires of us without imitating what is done by others. Consequently, we ought not to make it our duty to do every edifying action we see others do. The young solitary was blamed by the saint as negligent, although he did not do as much himself.

How wise and solid an instruction for directors of souls, well to discern the strength and attraction of each, in order to direct them according to the measure of the *gift of Christ Jesus*: To be careful how they subject those under their charge to a routine of conduct, or fear to find them more perfect or fervent than themselves, to prescribe for them rules they do not themselves observe, or to reprove them for failings from which they themselves are not exempt by their own acknowledgment. The solitary was condemned by him who was his inferior in practice and who does not reject his own judgment.

Modesty worthy of a saint to a saint! Admirable discernment which teaches that though we may do more works than the perfect, they will not insure our perfection, if we do not do all that we might do, or which God requires of us. Admirable instruction: teaching us to listen with simplicity to what our Directors may say to us without any examination of what they do themselves.

3.

Hold your heart then in Peace, and always be prepared to make strong exertions to support the works of God in the service of God. Understand nothing beyond your strength, approve whatever good you may see done, consider with complacency whatever may present itself to your mind, not imitating those, however, who while they amuse themselves with contemplating the extent of the heavens and the beauty of the stars are in danger of losing their way and falling into the precipice.

Busy yourself with the duties of your calling and the care of your soul. Praise and admire the Saints without either the vanity to think yourself like them, or the presumption to imitate them. Their example should have no other influence on you than to inspire you with more fidelity to your duties, and the measure of grace given to you. Go not out of your sphere; you will only err at random, for although the sun darts its rays at a great distance, the moon must still keep its place in order to receive its light, and would gain nothing by its endeavors to approach it.

Do not then undertake to imitate all the actions of the Saints, nor even the language they have used. It was an expression of their heroic sentiments, and yours are far inferior to theirs. Should you affect to speak like these great souls while yours is yet in its human weakness, you will either be guilty of untruth if you deceive others, or fall into error, if you deceive yourself. High and sublime language, contrasted with common and careless conduct, form a ridiculous opposition very injurious to piety.

Article Three

Moderation in the exercise of virtue

1.

It is only by combatting courageously, and bearing away the victory that we can deserve to be crowned; but there are crowns of different value, as there is more or less difficulty in winning them. Prudence should direct us to avoid those combats which are dangerous to our weakness, and we should never endanger the peace of our heart without necessity. You aspire to the highest perfection, and the good you find most difficulty in attaining is the only one that can satisfy you? Laudable resolution, and necessary even to the advancement you desire; but do not begin where you ought to finish, nor value yourself on a heroism which in a beginner is only presumption. Your vine is yet only in blossom. You may exercise yourself in catching the little foxes which hide themselves under it, and will certainly injure them; but do not go forth imprudently to seek the wild boars of the forest who will first overthrow you and then root out your plant.

Begin by surrounding the plant with a good wall in which you may enclose yourself to cultivate it and prevent the passing travellers from treading it down. Your heart is your fortress, if you will take the command over it, and establish the reign of tranquility and discipline. Keep the door well closed, and repulse the enemy with vigor and regularity. Count this a great deal and do not run the risk by an imprudent sally like the priests of Israel, of a defeat in which you will perish, or of being routed from your post which you will not easily recover (1 S 4).

2.

But in this, much discernment must be used; we must learn both to advance and retreat in this spiritual war, which at proper times requires as much prudence as resolution; retreats are as prejudicial as attacks when made at improper times. To avoid an enemy when we could vanquish him is losing a victory. To encounter the enemy when we should avoid him is running great risk.

We do not speak here of the impure spirit to whom we should never expose ourselves. We must always turn our back on Sodom, and not look at it *even at a distance,* not even to conceive a horror for its conflagration. But if it is necessary to fly from this spirit, it is also necessary to resist others, and some we must even provoke to the conflict. He who instead of subduing his enemy tries only not to be overcome by avoiding all occasions of gaining the prize will never acquire any virtues.

Great discretion is needful, says St. John Climacus, to know when, in what encounters, and how far we should fight against sin, in the occasions to which we may be exposed, and when we should wisely retire from the combat. If discretion is of great consequence, the practice of it is no less difficult, and the saint who teaches its necessity does not give us the means, although we may say he indicates it by treating almost immediately, holy peace; in truth, this interior peace is a near and ever-present rule enabling us to discover those enemies which we should combat with vigor, from those we should shun with prudence. If the temptation violently agitates you, if you lose the peace of your soul, if much care and time are required to recover it, do not expose yourself to this shock, as you will never come off without loss. Avoid it as much as possible until, being exercised by small conflicts, you will be able to gain great victories.

If only your interest was to be consulted, to overcome yourself in great occasions would certainly be the most advantageous; but as your strength must also be calculated, great occasions are the most critical without prepossession and without timidity. If necessary, avoid encountering a powerful enemy rather than expose yourself to be overcome, or at least troubled, exhausted and disheartened by a violent and obstinate resistance. But at the same time do not fail to combat by running away, and by astounding yourself for your little courage. Gain by humility what you might have gained by strength if you had overthrown your enemy; yet, propose for yourself that one day with the assistance of God, and a frequent practice of virtue to perform what is now too difficult to accomplish. Let us come to a more evident and detailed practice, as examples will realize precepts.

3.

My reputation is attacked by the darts of calumny which I could repel without much pain, but through my silence they will become extended and confirmed. What an occasion to destroy this fund of self-love, which under such excellent pretenses makes me so greedy of esteem, and so nice in point of honor. If I were strong enough to support these arrows which pierce me, my corruption would soon disappear; but I feel an extreme weakness and my heart is overcome. I can no longer pray or meditate. I have entirely lost my peace of soul and nothing assures me that it will return with the reputation which has been unjustly taken from me. I tremble at my want of virtue. I ask myself if I expect to acquire it without practicing it, or if I wait to practice it until I feel no repugnance for it; if it is by always postponing or delaying that we advance towards heaven, or by going forward despite all obstacles. But I treat myself on this occasion as I would treat a weak and timid invalid.

Touched with compassion, I defer the operation until he is more courageous and has gained strength; yet, I still exhort him to comply and to prepare for it, since his life depends upon it. Only one ingenuous and simple word would be sufficient to discover my innocence; I say it, and in saying it, I accept at least the humiliation proceeding from it, in my eyes and in those of virtuous persons who are surprised to see the limit of my patience.

4.

A person is so much opposed to me that every time we meet I am treated in a most cruel and harsh manner. I feel that I am not yet strong enough to suffer this affront with sufficient tranquility. My fund of self-love causes violent agitations in me which deprive me of peace. I avoid meeting with the person when I perceive an utmost irritation and when I can avoid it without scandal or inconvenience. But I find my strength increasing. I meet my adversary and take upon myself all the weight of this contradiction. Thus St. Francis at first fled from the unjust anger of his father; but fortified in his retreat, he discovers himself without fear to the greatest excess of his fury.

5.

I have received a grievous affront, though I am not insensible to it. God gives me grace not to be troubled; I use it according to the designs of God and the necessities of my soul; I willingly accept it and thank God for having permitted it. I pray for the one who has procured me this occasion to confound my self-love. I examine the injury I have endured, fix all my intentions on it, and in these moments, I sincerely acknowledge that I have merited this humiliation a thousand times for other reasons, if not precisely from the one who now occasions it.

But what this affront has not caused in me, the reflection which follows does. The idea which I recall moves me sensibly, troubles me and destroys my peace. I do not feel inclined to engage again with an enemy already vanquished, or to contend for a victory already obtained. I renew with simplicity the interior acceptation of this affront, and I turn all my endeavors to dissipating the remembrance of it. St. Francis acted in this manner when he felt his inclination to piety opposed by an inclination to covetousness; he resolved to turn his mind from this object by avoiding all thoughts of it.

This is the prudence of the saints; but our presumptuous temerity does not agree with these wise temperaments. It always desires the glory of seeing its enemies at its feet and never the humiliation of shunning the combat.

But what is the consequence? We fatigue ourselves in combatting and often without reason employ our efforts against those whom we have already vanquished and enslaved. Often, we also oppose and fight against phantoms and daydreams which will never be realized. In these vain debates against trifling faults, we lose our peace which never dwells in a tumultuous soul.

6.

Finally, we should never trouble our peace of soul by forced practice of virtue. Let us go by degrees in these difficult paths, however slowly we advance. We will make great progress, if we still go on, says Saint Francis de Sales (Ep. 47, L. 4). If we are not watchful over ourselves in these slippery paths, we are in danger of making many false steps and of falling at last into the precipice.

The saints have always feared walking hastily in these narrow paths of virtue, as we would tremble for an imprudent person who would run on the borders of an abyss where he should rather crawl on hands and feet, according to the example of the wise Jonathan (1 K:1) They have considered these sudden advances, only as riches quickly amassed and soon spent. A beginner who wishes to excel in everything, at first pushes forward without taking the least rest, and runs like a giant while yet he is only a child in virtue. God grant that he may do this as much through diffidence of himself as through want of strength and experience.

Indeed, I see him advancing rapidly, but I also see that this impetuosity will not carry him very far. He soon feels fatigued, he stops, and to stop in the path of virtue is to go back, while he who follows afar off by regular steps will leave him behind. Only those who come from heaven on earth should run like giants, but we who come from the bosom of the earth to go to heaven, we should walk with precaution and spare our strength. It is always, therefore, a real loss to trouble your soul by excessive but deceitful zeal in the advancement of virtue.

CHAPTER V

Of Interior Peace in Temptations

ARTICLE ONE

Interior peace is a very efficacious means to resist the most violent temptations; and the enemy gains not a little over us when he succeeds in making us lose it.

1.

If the love of God can excite irregular commotions in our souls which we must allay, the horror for evil and the vivacity of the temptations which brings it to view, oftener causes more dangerous troubles which we must suppress. Our weakness makes us more susceptible of fear which trifles and discourages the heart, than imprudent ardor which inflames and transports it. We can never have too much self-possession, nor arm ourselves too strongly against impressions of fear in violent temptations. It is a powerful means to avoid surprises, to resist attacks, to repair losses, to prepare the mind for receiving that heavenly light so necessary in these dark moments. The enemy is disconcerted when he finds we appear firm and confident, that far from gaining any advantages, he loses in tempting us; that we always become more humble by the simple and tranquil thought of our weakness, and more accustomed to use the strength given from above; that we always possess our peace with more merit and finally that our infirmity is fortified by all the efforts he uses to discourage us, as the reed is nourished by the same torrent that agitates it.

2.

You have overcome a grievous temptation, and behold you are extremely satisfied to have frustrated all the hopes of your enemy? You are deceived. If he has not gained as much as his malice wished, he has at least obtained all he hoped for, because you have come from the combat troubled, dissipated and your strength exhausted. He did not flatter himself that you would immediately fall into the precipice he presented to you; he saw you even too far from danger, and too well supported by the hand of God; he only expected to frighten you by showing you the depth of this abyss. But he did not despair to lead you into it afterwards, if it were only by the giddiness which he hopes your present trouble will create.

He attacks your heart, as sometimes enemies are attacked in the fort, not to subdue them, but only to draw them out, and to defeat them more easily in the open country. You are beside yourself? This is all the demon promised himself in his first attempt. Take care that he does not proceed as well in the second — if you do not hasten to take back from him again a profound peace — the advantage he had gained over you.

3.

It is certainly not subduing a temptation to come from the combat full of trouble which is of itself a great temptation. Nothing arises from interior trouble but melancholy thoughts to discourage us: obscenity, sorrow, melancholy, envy, jealousy, suspicion and discouragement. All are then revived, and reunite in us and against us. Thus the excessive fear of one temptation awakens almost all the others because trouble disturbs the depth of the soul, and all that was at rest within us arises, as the dregs at the bottom of the cask mixes immediately with the wine when it is moved. In this condition, we only perceive God in a confused manner; we can neither discern our distance from Him , or our access to Him; and like the disciples of Jesus, we take Him sometimes as for a spirit which deceives us, and sometimes for a phantom which affrights. We no longer know ourselves; we neither find our peace of soul, nor the delicacy of our thought, the propriety of our ideas, the vivacity of our sentiments, nor the firmness of our resolutions.

In short, we no longer know where we are, and we will only possess ourselves again by calming our uneasiness, and diverting ourselves from it by the contempt of everything that causes it, and by retiring within ourselves. This is the only means of dispelling the clouds which oppose the happy serenity.

But the temptation is horrible; it makes an impression on you; you feel an inclination for evil, but do not mind it. Be tranquil during the combat since you are not yet wounded. You will expose yourself to mortal wounds, if you do not retain your self possession. The impression is a sentiment which humbles you, not a consent which makes you guilty. This inclination is an infirmity of your nature and not a disorder of your will. The horror and infamy of this thought which so much affrights you ought to encourage you. The more horrible it is, the less dangerous for you and the more you fear it, the less reason you have to fear.

How can you love that which you even fear to see? And how is it possible that God who only reproaches us for a fault voluntarily loved should condemn you for a thought that afflicts and pains you?

On temptations of blasphemy

1.

It is a frightful blasphemy against interior peace the enemy suggests to you, the most impious and infamous that hell can invent! Without emotion, recognize the traits the malice of your enemy employs, and not the corruption of your heart. A favorable supposition on the corruption of the heart is that, perhaps, it never produced anything like it, even when its greatest dissipation might have caused it to utter all the evil it contained.

Another very consoling supposition for you is that the demon who afflicts you certainly does not reckon you among his own whom he cares not to disturb. He hates you mortally, hopelessly despairing to torment you in the other world. Knowing that he cannot conquer you, he endeavors to satisfy himself in this world. He tries, at least, to intimidate you, and not being able at first to afflict you, he attempts to fatigue and weaken you, in order to subdue you afterwards to his advantage when you are exhausted from struggling with these phantoms.

But after the Son of God made man was tempted by the greatest of all crimes, which is to adore the devil and to acknowledge him as His God, Jesus rejected this temptation only by answering the tempter peaceably: "It is written you will adore the Lord your God and Him only will you serve." Weak creature! nourished by corruption, should you be surprised that you are susceptible to some infamous suggestion? Should the horror you have of it trouble you? Are so many efforts to repel it necessary?

On temptations against purity

1.

A thought contrary to purity afflicts you; your trouble is super-fluous, but it does not surprise me. Those kinds of temptations are in the number of those with which timid souls are more frequently attacked. They perceive that the imperfect character of human nature either produces or gives rise to them; they take pleasure in them; the more pure they are, the more afflicted they will be to experience those impure impressions. St. Paul himself who so patiently suffered the most dreadful persecutions and the most cruel treatment could not help complaining to God of the attacks of Satan, and often prayed to be delivered from them.

Everything concurs to make the temptation violent and capable of troubling a modest person: the mind, memory, imagi-nation, natural inclinations, all unite against it. Thoughts are importunate and seem to stick to the soul wishing to repel them. Images are lively and seductive; they add novelty to the charms of voluptuousness. What shall I say? The flesh joins with the mind and soul finding itself between these two enemies, knows not which it shall combat or contend with: the one remains in perfect liberty, while it is maintaining combat with the other.

Dreadful situation! But it ought neither trouble your timid soul, nor cause these convulsive corporal agitations which, far from dissipating bad thoughts, would alone be sufficient to create them. This agitation which you suffer in yourself is sufficient to cause the impression which afflicts you. The more violent the inclination, the more firm you should be not to fall; the more impure the spirit which assaults you, the less you should contend with him, as you would sully your mind by the combat.

Turn your back upon him, forget that he is behind you, make no reply to his shameful proposals, and do not listen to what he says to you interiorly. Occupy your mind with some holy and consoling thoughts and your body with some moderate exercise, and remain quiet.

2.

When your enemy is gone, do not recall him to find out the strokes he has given you, if you have resisted them so well as not to have received any wound. This would be to renew the combat with new danger; your enemy preserves all his strength, while you are weakened by the first shock. How many has the devil not deceived by these means? He turned to their disadvantage those very scruples which had made them almost inaccessible to evil. He thus insensibly weakened those whom he attacked and finally conquered them by making them recall incessantly those seductive thoughts to examine if they had been seduced by them.

Forget then the kind, the occasion, and the duration of the combat, and even the perplexities it occasioned. If afterwards, it is necessary to take some means to tranquilize the alarmed and timid conscience, let the means be less in a follow-up examination which would be equally dangerous, so that the judgment might be favorable; that by considering these great principles that we can never really love what still we fear to love, that anything which wearies is not pleasing; that it is not the thought but the consent which makes the sin; that the more violent the conflict is the more evident is the resistance; that what we suffer from the impression of the evil is a subject of merit for us, and that commonly in timid persons accustomed to discern sin, a doubt if they have fallen is a presumption and almost a certainty that they have not yielded at least to mortal sin. Venial sins in this matter ought rather to be the subject of our sorrow and precaution than of our rigorous examination and detailed confessions.

On temptations of vain glory

1.

Another kind of temptation which generally brings trouble to the heart is the thoughts and sentiments of vain glory. We know that this vice is infinitely displeasing to God, that it is the poison of all virtues, that it alone is capable of losing the most holy souls, that it ruins the merit of good works and even turns them to a subject of condemnation.

We know all this; we recall it, and the devil thoroughly proud of himself does not omit exaggerating its malice; everything is pleasing to him, if he can only bring trouble into souls whose holy repose he sees with the most obstinate resentment. The snare is subtle, and it is rare that we are not caught in it. Who could imagine that we can fear variety too much, and that the father of pride conceals himself even under the veil of humility? We use no moderation in this exercise of virtue to avoid the opposite precipice; we make the greatest efforts to plunge ourselves into our own nothingness. We multiply the most melancholy and frightful reflections until, cast down by their weight, we think ourselves humble because we are dejected. This is not assuredly a good means of rejecting these temptations; but rather proper to trouble the peace of our soul.

A contemptuous look of your enemy and of yourself; a prudent forgetfulness of all that your self-love seems to find good in you; an attentive fidelity, without contention, to give to God the glory of all the talents He has bestowed upon you which you cannot deny that you possess; exactness in renouncing all vain desires of esteem and to retrench as much as possible all that would attract it; care to humble yourself with simplicity, for your pride is sufficient to destroy it, and to preserve at the same time our humility and peace of soul.

2.

We dare not ordinarily address our prayers to God in this grievous situation, because we are filled with confusion for our vanity which augments our melancholy and dejection. This is an illusion.

Turn yourself towards God with simplicity and love and He will fill your heart with consolation; look upon your temptations rather as an infirmity than as malice because your will is free; discover it with confidence and simplicity to the sovereign physician of your soul. Say to Him ingenuously: "Lord, him whom thou lovest is sick; is in a kind of delirium, look upon the wandering of my imagination and the excess of my folly. I think myself everything that I am not, and I think myself nothing else than what I really am. Theft is joined to the enjoyment; I appropriate to myself unjustly what you confided to me, after having foolishly attributed to myself what you did not bestow on me.

"*My God, preserve me in this double wandering, give me a just discernment of my poverty and your bounties; do not suffer me to exaggerate the talents which you have given me, nor to deprive you of the glory of which you are so justly jealous; take care yourself of your goods which are in unworthy hands. You even see me like Judas tempted to turn to my profit and advantage what had been given to me for your service.*"

If the thoughts of vain esteem and of vain complacency return again with importunity, a simple return towards God will be an abridged renewal of these humble and pious sentiments and a sufficient disavowal of the contrary impressions.

On temptations against faith

1.

Here, we should not forget the temptations against faith which are the most capable of staggering souls because they strike at the very foundation of a person's interior. A soul attacked by them is so much the more troubled because what is its resource in other temptations is precisely the cause of them. How exposed is the soul to the darts of the enemy? The soul combats against him for his shield and buckler; it no longer has the strength which gives the lively conviction that it is combatting for justice; it is no longer a temptation clearly known for which it combats, but an impression which even conscience makes it fear to act.

The complexity is great, and it is difficult; it is very rare that one does not lose his/her peace of soul in it; but how shall one act? Shall they reason and examine? This is not the time for it. Believe without examining and without reasoning? But is it absolutely without reasoning and without examining that we can calm reason in revolt against itself and an alarmed conscience? To believe because we are resolved to believe is capriciousness. Believe because one has been brought up in this belief? This is prejudice. Believe today because we believed yesterday? This is habit or custom. Believe because learned persons and people without number believe the same? This is human faith. To believe because by our own lights we judge it to be founded on the word of God? This is a presumption which prefers its own discernment to that of others; it is a source of heresies very far from being a resource in temptations.

To believe because the Catholic Church believes it and that God has revealed it? This is the only way of coming out of this labyrinth. Happy they who can attain to this and hold to it; still more, if the temptation is against the Church and divine revelation. But if we see no more of the first principles than of the last conclusions, if religion entirely disappears in the storm, the whole is lost. We float like children, in certain loss of the peace of our souls, and a great risk of our faith.

2.

We see by the above that those who give to souls tempted against faith, only the remedy of blindly submitting to revealed truths, and to disavow the impressions contrary to them, either do not give them a remedy as great as the evil, or they do not sufficiently explain its use. A remedy which being centered in the idea it presents does not radically cure the wound of the heart, but always leaves a fund of uneasiness; a remedy which may be turned to poison and does not clearly show itself since many opposers of the truth exact from their adversaries a blind submission. Finally, a remedy which does not suppose a true knowledge of the evil, which, however, is the first step we should take to obtain a perfect cure.

We must not, therefore, reason during the temptation, but we must dwell on serious reflections upon what we believe, and on the motives we have for this belief. We must be discreet in wisdom, but we must also be prudent and reasonable in submission. We must obey without reply, but we must know to whom we obey, and by what authority they claim our obedience, without which we run the risk of not obeying well, even in obeying those to whom we owe obedience.

3.

We must then be acquainted with religion, at least to a certain degree and as far as we are able. We must first notice its exterior supports and its interior economy; we must know that there is but one Religion; that it is of divine institution, as is its purpose; that it is the only means of knowing God, as much as He wishes to be known, because He only makes Himself known through it; that He has the authority to lead us and the light to enlighten our path. We must be instructed that it is the Catholic Church which goes back to the very church of the Israelites and, by it and the patriarchs, ascends even to the very first beginnings of that worship and law which is the only depository of this religion, the lawful interpreters of the Scriptures and the faithful witness of revelation; that by a necessary and final consequence, it is no longer permitted to reason, we must listen to the Catholic Church with an entire submission, however difficult the doctrine which it presents to our belief may be.

These promises are so clear that they can penetrate the most narrow minds, if they are presented in their true light, by those charged to teach them. If anyone should think it is not right that the simple faithful soul should reason so much, let him take notice that those who are not led at least implicitly by these degrees, to believe the holy doctrine, believe often without knowing why, and, as it were, by random. To what temptation is he not exposed? What then shall be his resource? If he is not tempted, does not his tranquility originate from his indifference? What an injury does he not do to religion which he always fears to search into; for which he can give no reason and to which he is, perhaps, only attached because of his birth, his education, or rather fate decreed him to believe it.

4.

But these great principles once fixed and sufficiently penetrated into a soul who knows there is a time to see and examine without doubting, and a time to submit and to silence reason though without imprudence; that the first must be done without temptation and trouble, and the last is the business of almost all our life; that Religion in its extent is evident and clear; that its principles are linked together by so necessary a connection that it is impossible to abandon a single one without unhinging and destroying the rest.

That we cannot deny one single article of faith without being led by degrees and by necessary consequences to deny the existence of a church, of a religion, and even of a God, that what is now the cause of one's perplexity in the moment of trial, was the object of his fervent adorations, his enraptured meditations, of his holy delights in time of peace; that though the faith in its exterior appearance and in its preliminaries is a reasonable obedience, it is in itself an obedience of reason; a soul, I say, who knows all its truths and possesses itself in time of temptation finds itself too strongly grounded in faith to be troubled.

It respects the darkness spread over the face of the abyss and it descends into it without fear, undaunted on the footsteps of faith. The soul is firm and confident because it knows in whom it confides. Not only that it is not troubled to see itself in this deep obscurity, but it even feels that the brightest day of spiritual joy would never afford it so solid a consolation. This is the way to preserve our peace in temptations against faith without which we should expose ourselves to lose both.

Article Six

On temptations against hope

1.

After the temptations against faith of which we have just spoken, those against hope follow naturally in this place. They are all very capable of troubling the interior peace of a soul who only reposes in God, because this person knows God's goodness, and enjoys His presence, although He is not visible to him/her during their lifetime, the person hopes to see and possess Him in the eternity of the next life. As long as the just have their support in a firm hope, they will not be moved.

But if this support fails or is shaken, how can they keep themselves firm? The fear of God, once their consolation, now no longer moderated by humble confidence, becomes only their torment. It was a tender attentive Master who introduced and protected this hope; now, He becomes a rigid examiner who will make him suffer more than he could from a declared enemy.

The imaginary traits of God's anger which this unhappy person continually augments will pierce him to the very soul, and will destroy all his charism and interior spirit. He dares not seek his consolation in God because he imagines it is God who has kindled this fire which consumes him. He will seek for it among men, but he will find few who will understand his pains and among those who do, few will commiserate him, and still fewer who are able to appease them. Many will even augment them by exaggerating his faults or by irritating his imagination which should be pacified.

The darkness of his mind increases in proportion to the distress of his heart and the farther he goes from the path of peace, the more difficult he will find his return to it. To increase the evil, this temptation, the worse of all others, is what it least appears to be. He imagines, on the contrary, that it is a strong faith which makes him feel the weight of these terrible truths which strike him.

2.

But these dreadful pangs are far from being what we imagine them. Faith is the foundation of hope, and the latter is the more firm and consoling, in proportion as the faith is lively and animated. We always see joy, consolation, confidence and peace augment in proportion, as we are more persuaded of God's love for us, of the power of His grace, of the efficacy of the blood of Jesus

Christ, and of the virtue of sacraments which contain the price of it and which apply its merits. All essential, original and clear truths which we neglect in order to think of others more remote and even impenetrable, as of the uncertainty of our predestination, the depths of God's judgments, the severity of His justice, truths of which we should rarely think, and only to abate our presumption and excite fervor.

Frequent reflections on terrifying truths often become a temptation, and a temptation commonly least suspected, but easily discerned, if properly reflected on. It brings trouble, weakness, discouragement, distance from God in our soul which could be only effected by our enemies.

God, on the contrary, always excites in us a sweet calm, a modest joy, a firm resolution to serve Him even in the strongest impressions which His grandeur makes upon our souls, in the most humiliating repentance which He causes in us, and in the sharpest remorses with which He inspires us. The more dangerous, turbulent and opposed to our peace of soul this temptation is, the more we should resist its approach, and weaken it during its intervals by the following reflections and practices taken mostly from St. Francis de Sales, who, having a long time experienced these great afflictions, sensibly communicates, as he says himself, the melancholy state of these afflicted souls (St. Francis de Sales, Ep. 30-31, L. 5).

3.

We have already said that we should occupy ourselves seldom and only on particular occasions with certain truths of religion which frighten and overwhelm us. Timid persons subject to temptations against hope ought even prudently to reflect on those which surprise and strike them most. Of the vast extent of eternity in which we are lost, of the infinity of God who is an abyss without end or limit; of the little we can do to merit this immense weight of glory to which we aspire, and of the little we do of this *little* which we should do, there is but one step between terror and distrust. The most evident mysteries, the most practicable truths, the simplest maxims should be the common occupation of timid souls, as yet but little advanced in virtue.

4.

It is so rare that thoughts of predestination touch the heart and excite piety, so much as they surprise the mind and irritate the imagination, that the most enlightened directors of souls do not allow them without the greatest precaution, and absolutely forbid them in those who are agitated by the above-mentioned temptations. What advantages, say they, could you derive or rather what a loss is it for you to employ that time in thinking with so much melancholy on your predestination, which should be employed entirely in working courageously to merit it? There is nothing, you say, which you would not do, if you knew you were one of the elect. Do now all you would do then, and you will be more certainly one of them than if an angel had revealed it to you.

The fear of reprobation which afflicts you is entirely frivolous in its excess and in its inquiries into futurity. Did God, who made known to many saints during their mortal life that they were predestined, ever put it into the mind of a reprobate that he was to be condemned? In truth, this knowledge and this thought is useless. You will be one day either of the number of the blessed or you will not repent, say these wise directors to those persons who lose their time, health, and devotion in making these reflections, as useless as they are terrifying.

If you are to be numbered among the blessed, you will be less blessed in proportion to the time you have spent in thinking about it. If you are not among the blessed, it will be only through your own fault. And is it not already one of them to wish to penetrate into the judgments of God, to search the depths of His counsels, and to discover in spite of Him what He wishes to conceal, instead of adoring His majesty, praising His wisdom, enjoying His presence, and accomplishing His will? Abandon then these thoughts which only serve to make you suffer even in this world a portion of the torments of reprobation and to make you almost merit them by your excessive fear and opposition to the will of God in allowing these thoughts to occupy you.

5.

A tender piety is very proper to comfort souls afflicted by these temptations. Interior fervor always mitigates the bitterness of this poison which the enemy breathes in our hearts. The sight, the taste and still more the practice of good works cheer and encourage more than the most consoling reflections we could prescribe in this state. Often, these ideas deliver the soul already overpowered with affliction to a dry meditation and melancholy void, where the former thoughts are more powerful than those one wishes to substitute, because they occupy the same place, are strengthened by having long dwelt there, and excite more lively and dangerous impressions.

If we wish for reflections, and in truth, they are necessary because the seat of the evil is in the mind and in the imagination where the remedy must be applied, let them be strong, short and earnest. We must go to the mind through the heart, because all other avenues are closed. Interior movements, provided they are not forced, nor too long continued, generally produce a fire which enlightens the mind, while at the same time it warms the heart.

Therefore, instead of farfetched, slow and difficult arguments, I would advise those persons often to make use of animated and consoling reflections, most proper to dispose and drive away the enemies. We will furnish here a few affectionate and elevating thoughts which may be used to advantage, but which should always yield to those that experience teaches them would be more effective, or those suddenly produced by their own heart.

"It is in you, my God! that I have hoped; I shall never be con-

founded. *To you, proud and obstinate spirits, infamous demons, to you be reprobation and despair and not to a penitent and humbled soul, who trembles incessantly for the evil it does. How great is the virtue of your blood, my* **Savior Jesus.** *The whole world finds in it a superabundant redemption. It would also be sufficient for a million others were they capable of repentance and salvation as I am.*

"*Oh! though my sins should be a thousand times more enormous and numerous, my evil inclinations more violent and dreadful, my daily faults more frequent and willful, I will fear nothing so much as excessive fear.*

"*Doubt of thy mercy? No, Lord, though my falls should every day become greater, while I preserve the will to rise up again, while you still draw me by the desire of going to you, I will never despair either of your grace to convert me, nor of your mercy to pardon me. How sweet it is to hope in the Lord God! Hell itself would no longer be what it is, if the least ray of this hope could pierce its darkness; it alone can deprive me of so great a good, and the cloud of despair can arise only from its abyss.*"

6.

Devotion to the Blessed Virgin Mary is a singular and great resource in temptations against hope. It is a powerful means of salvation, a fruitful source of all kinds of good and even a mark of predestination according to St. Anselm and many other Fathers of the Church. "*If the remorses of your conscience and the fear of God's judgments throw you into a deep melancholy,*" says St. Bernard, "*if the enormous weight of your crimes draws you towards the abyss of despair, turn yourself towards Mary, implore her assistance; you will soon receive joy, confidence and peace. You are a sinner? Mary is this mysterious ladder by which sinners ascend to Heaven, the gates of which they had shut against themselves. Though a sinner like you, yet, I am full of confidence because I find in her the most powerful motives to excite it.*"

Before St. Bernard, St. Ephrem had called her the hope of those who had no other hope, and after him, St. Thomas [Aquinas] gives to her in union with the Church the praises of wisdom, presents her to us as the foundation of all our hope in life and grace.

It is then very useful in these moments of trial and affliction to have recourse to Mary. But in a simple affectionate and confident manner by pronouncing her name, looking at her image, thinking of the virtues she practiced, of the glory she possesses, and of the tender truly maternal love she has for us. Address her with the prayers of the Church: "*Mary, Mother of Grace and Mercy, protect us against our enemy*"; or the other recited habitually every day without spirit and without reflection, but which in itself is full of consolation and which, above all, in time of temptation becomes personal, interesting and animated: "*Holy Mary, Mother of God, pray for us* now"; or these three short and animated words — "*our life, our sweetness, our hope*"; or, say to her in the most violent temptations what young Tobias said to the Angel Raphael: "*Alas! this infernal monster is ready to devour me; he seizes and drags me to his abyss; powerful protectress hasten to assist me.*"

If the state of your soul were as melancholy and desperate as that of the celebrated Theophilus sold to the devil not only by wanderings and disorders, but by choice and express contract written with his hand and blood, like him you will find in your confidence with Mary, *Hope, Grace and Salvation.*

7.

The love of God, above all, is very efficacious in bringing back peace to a soul agitated by these temptations because it dilates and strengthens the heart, inspires with generous sentiments, and banishes that kind of fear which makes for unhappiness and is only fit for slaves. Take, for instance, the well known example of Saint Francis de Sales. The enemy, jealous of the peace of his soul, and the progress he made in virtue, put it in his mind that it was useless to mortify his senses, since he was not among the number of the elect. A very afflicting thought for a saint who was much troubled by it. In vain, he seeks for relief. He carries everywhere along with him the image of his reprobation imprinted on his mind, and feels in some degree its effects.

The God of goodness, who calls sinners, loves the most obstinate, consoles and serves the penitent, is now to him only a severe judge who condemns him to eternal torments for the imperceptible stains of his life, or through the impenetrable depths of His judgments.

But this God whose judgments he so much fears in these terrible moments, he has always loved, and loves Him still. The enemy who strikes him with useless and troublesome impressions cannot weaken this generous and consoling love which affords him a powerful resource. "Well," he says, in the midst of this dark cloud which surrounds him, "If I am so unhappy as not to be able to contemplate this infinite beauty during all eternity, I will at least praise and adore it during my whole life. The more I fear not to love forever a God so worthy of being loved, the more I will redouble my endeavors to love Him more and more while I live." This courageous and fervent resolution of purest love is like a flash of lightning which darts a sudden light into his soul and a clap of thunder which overthrows his enemy.

8.

Excessive fear of our weakness and of the temptations to which we may be exposed is a fruitful source of vain terrors. *We will never possess peace as long as we fear to lose it.* You who find in the present every motive of consolation, will you seek fears in futurity? Is repose a burden to you? "Why?" you ask. While each day is sufficient for its own evil, you collect in a moment what is spread throughout a lifetime. You unite by your anticipations, temptations which God only wanted you to subdue singly. This is the most dangerous of all temptations. It is very difficult not to yield to it; it is tempting God. It is drawing on yourself, enemies to whom He does not wish you to expose yourself at present: it is wishing to combat them alone and without help, thus exposing yourself to perish.

Limit yourself to the present moment and you will be tranquil; live upon your daily bread and think not of tomorrow. Do not trouble yourself about a distant futurity — you, who perhaps are at the last moment of your life.

If you have already overcome the temptations you feared, why could you not continue to overcome them? You only feel weakness because it is not the time of combat, but only of your imprudence. God gives grace to the occasion and present necessity, and not at all times and according to our whims. Samson of Israel was not seized with the spirit of God, except when monsters were to be overcome or there were enemies to combat. Had you formerly been overcome by those who now make you tremble, far from weakening yourself by fear you should strengthen yourself by all kinds of precautions.

Nothing can be more formidable to our enemies than a soul who unites a confidence in God to a contempt and diffidence of self. It was what they were forced more than once to confess to [one of the Desert Fathers,] the Abbot Moses: "Thou has vanquished us, Moses," they said to him, "and all our efforts against you are vain, because when we wished to humble you, in order to make you despair, you raise yourself up, and when we wanted to raise you that you may become vain, you humble and cast yourself down."

As the fear which only restrains our passions and excites our fervor is a *real good*, and that which tends only to afflict and deject us in order to take away our desire of spiritual things, and diminish the desire of our advancement can only be an evil and a very great evil, all our efforts will not be too great to destroy it. We can destroy it, however, by reflecting frequently that it cannot proceed from God, since it removes us from Him, and that it can only be the work of a malicious spirit, since it is so conformable to his designs.

We can destroy it by a tender devotion to God which elates the heart, mitigates its wounds, and puts the enemy to flight like the song of David that delivered Saul from the malicious spirit which tormented him (1 S 16). We can also destroy it by a confidence in God who desires our salvation more earnestly than we do ourselves. He so much wishes us to be convinced of this that He makes it a crime, and even a great crime to doubt it. He is as able to execute on us the designs of His mercy, as He is good in forming them in our favor. He is so anxious for our salvation that our loss seems to affect His happiness. Finally, we can destroy this fear by the knowledge and love of Our Lord, Jesus Christ, by a frequent participation of the Sacrament of His body; by meditations on these mysteries and the love which caused Him to work them for our salvation; a love which presses Him continually to consummate the work of our redemption by the baptism of His blood.

ARTICLE SEVEN

General maxims to preserve both innocence and peace in temptations

It would be an endless task to attempt enumerating the different kinds of temptation which may trouble the peace of our soul, but every kind can and will produce this bad effect unless guarded against by the following regulations or maxims:

Maxim 1.

We must not fear temptations too much, nor desire to be delivered from them with too much earnestness, because excessive fear would keep us in continual alarm; this of itself is sufficient to renew them by retracing the image they have left on the mind, and while it gives strength to the enemy, it will increase our weakness for the time of combat. We must be firmly persuaded that God will not permit us to be tempted beyond our strength; temptation never can hurt us if we do not yield to it. On the contrary, it produces the best effects in faithful souls; it humbles them, it awakens their watchfulness; it exercises their patience and their courage; it supports their fervor, recalls them to God, renders them compassionate to others and capable of advising them. For this reason, the saints, far from begging to be delivered from them, suffered them with joy, for in truth, each one we surmount merits for us a crown and furnishes us with arms for our combat, as Goliath furnished David with the sword which beheaded him.

Maxim 2.

We should not always oppose an earnest resistance to temptations, but substitute contempt for strength, if they do not yield to the first resistance. I cannot repeat too often that ordinarily it is owing to our violent resistance that we are overpowered with weariness and trouble. Our enemy is a child when we despise him and a giant when we fear him. We find in the life of St. Anthony [of the Desert] and other saints that legions of the enemy have been dispersed by a laugh of ridicule, or a sharp raillery. It is certain that temptations are much more easily conquered by the help of God with patience and gentleness than by a violent and angry resistance to distrust and impatience.

Maxim 3.

Our temptation should be made known to our director. We see in the lives of the saints and particularly of the Fathers of the Desert how great is the importance of this maxim, and in one of them a sorrowful example. He was violently tempted for the space of twenty years and could find no remedy until he told it to one of the elderly Fathers. The prince of darkness hates the light which shows him in his true colors and discovers the secret of the heart. This lion which roams through the night to seek and devour his prey, retires in the shades of darkness the moment the day appears. The father of pride, the lion, hates nothing so much as humility, which owns and admits its misery.

The opening of the heart becomes an outlet for the fire of temptation which remaining enclosed would keep it disordered and in continual agitations. But the director to whom the heart is opened must be well chosen or his want of experience may aggravate the wound, and the evil be increased by the very means which should lessen it.

Maxim 4.

It is also of importance not to multiply reflections which afflict the temptations themselves, such as their duration, violence, the danger of consenting to them, the happiness of those who are exempt from them; but rather: watch, pray, confide in God and avoid the occasion of them as far as prudence permits. St. Peter walked securely over the depths of the sea while he looked only on his divine master, but began immediately to sink when he cast his eyes on the waves and billows surrounding him.

Maxim 5.

Although prayer is, indeed, our great resource against temptation, yet other means are also necessary. What may seem very strange is that these means should be directly opposite, such as: labor, amusement, gaiety. For there are some imaginations which receive such lively and deep impressions that they carry them with them wherever they go. They remain with them until after impressions still stronger come to replace or efface them. In this case, it is evident that to recollect the mind is only a means of indulging images pictured upon it. Prayer of itself cannot be sufficient without additional means, and God wills us to use them in whatever may be effectual: an assiduous study, a work of attention, and succession of occupations with no other interval than absolute necessity; short and lively aspirations of the heart to God to entreat His help that peace of soul may be preserved in this dissipation intended only for withdrawing the temptation.

This method was successfully used by a wise solitary who relieved a young religious from a most obstinate temptation by continual occupation both of body and of mind, not leaving a moment for reflection. It is well known that this motive engaged St. Jerome in the study of Hebrew which challenged his mind to the limit of his patience. Those who are neither capable of application in study or continual labor may find a substitute in conversing with pious friends; in the contemplation of nature; a walk in the country, or whatever may contribute to dissipate that sadness so inseparably connected with the combat they endure.

                                    Maxim 6.

In time of temptation, we are generally led to take strong resolutions either to avoid or vanquish them even at the time they press hardest upon us. But this is precisely the moment when we should make no resolution, but such as we would make at any other time, or such as might reasonably be made by someone. The conduct we adopt and the regulation made in this time of agitation almost always partake of the trouble of our state, and being generally in extremes, creates new difficulties, either by imposing duties or practices above our state, in which, if we fail, we directly imagine that we are unfaithful to God.

Although God can never approve, much less exact the accomplishment of our imprudence, yet, should the temptation be renewed, we consider it a punishment for imaginary infidelities, and still more, should it be weakened and discouraged by the means intended to remedy the evil, it only contributes to double the effect.

Maxim 7.

Not only should we preserve our interior tranquility in the midst of temptation, but still further, should we begin to feel ourselves troubled, we should never express it outwardly by our gestures and inquietudes. To disconcert the enemy, we should also preserve our exterior tranquility by our outward appearance, and then, perhaps, the enemy only judging by the exterior may despair and give up his assault precisely at the moment we are ready to yield. Like a besieging enemy who has long endured a vigorous defense he imagines he may still meet with a stronger resistance and abandons the contest, without knowing the trouble and disorder which reigns within the walls.

CHAPTER VI

One must not be troubled even by the sins he commits.

1.

Here, indeed, we have need of confidence: you who cannot bear your sins while God supports them with so much patience. You will not hearken to a proposition of peace respecting your faults because you do not observe that it is peace with yourselves, not peace with sin of which we speak: A tranquil repentance at the very moment of your fall appears to you a contradiction and even an error. We know that we must hate evil and it would be a very great one to consider it with indifference; but is there no difference between that insensibility your reason fears, and the vexation, the trouble, and chagrin produced by your impatience? A humble and peaceable return towards God is equally distant from both these extremes.

"Peaceable return towards God," you will say, "must not sin

be struck at the root? Shall the publican dare to lift his head and enter within the sanctuary? Should he not remain on the pavement, strike his breast and consider the depths of his wounds and his misery?" In this question, I see only your attachment to your own ideas and your excessive ardor, but if possible hear me tranquilly.

2.

In the first place, sin must be struck at the root and be destroyed, it is true, but in doing this, is it necessary to destroy ourselves, trouble our reason, ruin our health and by the violence of our emotions derange our interior and exterior, and put it out of our power to follow the divine light or even to discern it? We must undoubtedly subdue our hearts, but can it not be effected without the expense of our peace?

We must examine the depths of our wounds, but must we increase and poison them by dint of opening them to discover their extent? The publican remaining at the entrance of the temple smiting his breast and keeping his eyes on the ground; yes, this is his place and his proper situation, but he is more peaceable in the humility of his repentance than the pharisee devoured by his problems and puffed up by his false justice. All true penitents have been like the converted publican in peace as soon as they have acknowledged themselves guilty.

The holy King Hezekiah recalls the years of his life in bitterness of heart, but this bitterness does not in the least alter his peace. David, indeed, often speaks of affliction and dread in his penitential psalms, but he acknowledges that this affliction is only the exterior of a penitent and afflicted soul, fitted with the joy of its confidence in God. Saint Mary, niece of Abraham the hermit, weeps over her sins. Ah! What sins! but she weeps for them, says the author of her biography in a great spirit of penance.

Does the simple and tranquil return towards God still appear difficult to you? Observe attentively that as sin is nothing but a separation from God to attach us to the creature, so, true conversion consists in turning from the creature to return to God, with a sincere repentance for having displeased Him, and a true resolution to satisfy Him for the past, and be more faithful for the future. All beyond this vexation, trouble, innumerable reflections on our falls, is but a remainder of our attachment to creatures, a refined self-love and an obstacle to our perfect conversion.

We must tremble at our faults, but our fear should not proceed from the natural sentiment which inspires a hatred of our imperfections, as this is only a source of impatience and trouble; we must tremble for them through our love for God, and through a desire of His glory, and our own salvation. You wish to return to God by detesting the creature which caused you to abandon Him; you should on the contrary begin by returning to God, and then your attachment to creatures will naturally cease.

3.

The sorrow of a soul, beside herself, or the sight of her repeated faults is far from being what she imagines it, that is, a *knowledge* of *herself* and *humility*. She sees herself confusedly in a disorder which affrights her, but which she cannot define, and she neither perceives the mercies of God on her, the seeds of virtue which He has sown in her, nor the interior motions He causes in her. Neither does she see the resistance she opposed to the temptation before she yielded to it, the regret she felt in yielding to it, nor the quickness with which she rose again from the fault.

She does not distinguish the happy inclination for piety which incessantly recalls her to it, which is a present from her God and a token of His love from that kind of fatality which caused her to contract evil inclinations in time of dissipation and that God, less attentive to her surprises than to her dispositions, looks upon them more as a misfortune than as a malice.

I dare even say not to alarm the soul more, but to discover the illusion concealed under this beautiful appearance of a knowledge of itself, that she does not see all the evil that a saint would perceive, more so without, however, losing his peace. Witness among others, St. Francis of Assisi who said and thought himself the greatest of all sinners and who was still always in a holy joy and a declared enemy of melancholy in himself and in others. If we are troubled at seeing the corruption of our heart, it is not because we know the extent of it, but because we see it in a false light. It is rather a confused view than a distinct knowledge.

Also this false knowledge of ourselves does not produce humility which should be the fruit of it. Often, we find persons who appear to think and say so much evil of themselves really filled with the idea of their own merit which occupies their thoughts incessantly. We see them troubled, indecisive, easily vexed, and in reality less humbled by the evil they find in themselves, than flattered with the knowledge they possess in discerning it. This trouble and fear are the work of the enemy who always proud of himself will swell the heart when he abates our courage. It is then, to express myself according to St. Teresa of Avila, a hellish humility which deprives us of confidence in God, and the peace of our souls.

4.

You lose courage at the sight of your relapses in opposition to your resolution. I expect much from your resolutions, if you keep them, despite your relapses. I dare affirm that the enemy has much less hopes from the resolutions than from the relapses, and if he earnestly tries to make you fall frequently into the same faults, it is to make you timid rather than criminal. He aims above all at your courage; he will be disconcerted, if you do not allow yourself to be afflicted. As a strong and proud enemy, often victorious, becomes at last intimidated when he sees him whom he had so often conquered and thrown down, always rise up again with new resolution and return upon him with fresh courage. Therefore, when you fall frequently during the day into the same faults, rise up as often with the same courage, and fear nothing as much as a want of hope.

Ah! Why should you not hope, since God still calls you. You feel a desire to go to Him of which He alone can be the author, and which would be yet more earnest, if you were less fearful. He is satisfied with the promise of your will despite your faults and imperfections. Hope much in God, and I will hope much for you in spite of your weakness. It is on His word that I hope to see hereafter the rapidity of your spiritual progress equal to the extent of your present miseries. Do not imagine that these maxims concern only a small number of chosen souls. They are applicable to all kinds of people.

Directors are so much accustomed to this, that they always expect more from these pious souls who, although they commit considerable faults, rise up again with renewed ardor, than from those who are exempt from those faults, but have not the resolution which precedes and follows them. They, indeed, see in the first a remaining weakness, but also always a new courage. They see the extraordinary efforts of the enemy to stop them, but also the particular assistance God grants them — a mark of predestination which does not escape their notice. These persons will never frustrate their hopes, if they do not yield to the snare of dissipation, or to that of discouragement. It is generally rare that they should have to wait a long time for the abundant fruits of their care and patience.

We see an example of this conduct in the life of the foundress of a religious house. Two aspirants presented themselves to embrace a monastic life. One of a disposition who could with a most tranquil air practice all the duties of a religious state and no fault of ill humor could be found in her. The other, on the contrary, was subject to both, but these defects were counterbalanced by a firm resolution to correct herself and attain perfection. This foundress sent away the former and received the latter to the great astonishment of those who could not discern like her, the different dispositions: the strength of the charm and the extent of grace; and who knew not that by much courage and strength we advance rapidly, although we fall very frequently; with much slowness, we advance very little, though we do not leave the road or make any blunders in it.

5.

Dositheus committed faults, but because he repaired them immediately without becoming discouraged, only a few years were necessary to make him a saint. St. Catherine of Siena also fell into some faults and as she mourned them before our Lord, He made known to her that her simple, prompt, lively and confident returns pleased Him more than her faults offended Him. All the Saints have committed faults, and sometimes the greatest have fallen into the most considerable, as David, St. Peter, St. Theophilus, and perhaps, they would never have been such great saints, if they had not fallen into faults and great ones. "All concurs for the good of the elect," says St. Paul; "even their sins," says St. Augustine. Yes, while a tepid soul turns into a snare and even into a sin, the little good that person does, a fervent soul turns to a means of sanctification, the very sins into which the person falls. Her infidelities augment her fervor as a large fire becomes more active by throwing only a little water on it. God who sees how useful these infidelities are, permits them by His providence, and pardons them with goodness.

God of mercy, you then sacrifice your glory to our good and you suffer us to become ungrateful, unfaithful, and guilty because you foresee that we will from thence become more humble, more circumspect and more holy.

6.

I am emphasizing this chapter, and my dwelling so long on it should make these uneasy penitents comprehend how much care their situation demands and how much reason I have to condemn their impatience. I multiply reflections because experience has taught me that though they are very necessary, they are very difficult to be made in a state in which we can scarcely profit by those of others; the mind being shut up by the most melancholy images and the heart oppressed by fear leaving scarcely any opening to light or to consolation. It is for this reason that I ask, in the first place, these persons to listen to me quietly and for a moment to appease all their alarms. Since in their situation, we cannot exact their obedience, I endeavor to enforce the necessity of it. Authority gives place to persuasion, and I shall then succeed to convince you that I command with reason, I am sure of commanding with success in a thousand other occasions without giving a reason for commanding.

Imagine, I say, these minds more dejected by their reflections than by their falls that this strong impression of fear and melancholy (which you call an impression of regret and repentance) is in you a production of the Holy Spirit? You dare not say it, or at least, you could not prove it. And I say the Holy Spirit is not, nor can be the author of it, and what I say, I prove. The true sentiments of repentance are always accompanied with the hope of pardon; hope is the source of all true joy, and you feel only an opposition to both. The remorse of conscience produced by God mitigates trouble; yours always augments it more and more.

God excites in us a desire of repairing our faults and you feel no other inclination than to abandon everything? A soul animated with holy repentance raises herself towards God who inclines towards her in order to give her the kiss of peace. Like Adam, a prevaricator, you fly His presence and would wish to hide from His looks. Excessive melancholy, namely, that which amounts to uneasiness and discouragement is so far from being an effect of true contrition that the Apostle will not suffer the incestuous Corinthian to yield to it even for a scandalous crime, and this, says St. Paul, not to fall into the snare of the enemy whose designs we know (2 Cor 2). For small faults you give yourself up to sorrowful and melancholy regrets, as useless as they are violent from the want of confidence. It is then, undoubtedly, the enemy who inspires this distressing repentance or, at least, who excites it to an excess.

7.

But what does this spirit of darkness say to you? Principally two things: the first without a doubt that you are not truly converted if you are still so weak; that it is not so easy to fall into evil that we have sincerely detested; that uprightness gives quite another consistency to the soul; that it is not so easy for the enemy to encroach upon a treasure protected as it is interiorly by the grace of God which inhabits it, and by His angels who surround it: a reasoning as false as it is seductive.

A soul who fears sin and avoids its occasions; who labors daily by spiritual exercises to fortify itself against temptations; who obviates the allurement of pleasure by mortification, the surprises of passion by vigilance, and all their efforts by prayer, this soul, I say, is truly converted; although not impeccable, she is generally in a state of grace, even when at times she falls.

The faults she commits occasionally are not of a nature to cause her to lose grace, or at least, they do not support the notion that this soul was not in the state of grace before committing them, and still less that a sincere repentance will not establish her in her former state. Nothing, on the contrary, more forcibly proves the favors of God in a soul than the desire to return to Him after an unhappy separation from Him. Nothing more clearly proves that He still dwells in the soul, than the interior reproaches felt by it for the slightest faults.

8.

Secondly, this spirit of darkness tells you that you will never correct yourself of your defects, since you fall so frequently into them, despite your strongest resolutions; that your bad habits are strengthened every day; that each of your falls increases the weight of your chains which finally you can neither break nor carry; that being so negligent in the first moments of fervor when all obstacles are generally overcome — a time when everything which opposes a rising zeal is broken through and destroyed. Nothing will stop you when the first spark of this fervor will be abated.

In fine, the demon will suggest to you that each of your faults is a diminution of that grace which was given to you, and will produce mutual coldness between God and you. Reasoning as vicious and false as the first. No, the habits of your faults are not strengthened by each of their returns; you fall through weakness, surprise or what remains of former habits which daily become less violent and less willful, but you rise up again by courage and reflections, by your desire for constant fidelity which is fortified by the soul's regrets of its continual infidelities. Faults of mere weakness preceded by a strong resistance, or committed without reflection and followed by a ready repentance leave scarcely a trace in the soul. It is a fire which we take in our hands and throw away immediately, and from which we receive scarcely any injury.

But what forms a true habit are the returns of your repentance: voluntary, deliberate, long supported and difficult, since they have to surmount the impression of recent sin, the weakness of propensity which it has left in the soul, the ascendance it has given to the enemy, the violence with which this cruel enemy pushes you on the brink of the precipice, and your own timidity which cannot recover its loss, but by the greatest effort.

Therefore, you can say in a true sense that you are strengthened by all your weaknesses: "When I am weak, it is then that I am strong" and that daily good habits gain the ascendancy over bad ones precisely by the occasions of these surprises caused in you by their miserable remains. What becomes then of your Communions, your prayers, your meditations, your austerities, and in a word, of your pious devotions? This is what the enemy does not speak to you about, for it is in his interest to remove you from your serious reflections.

9.

Another diabolical error and illusion: a beginner filled with fervor whom God strongly attracts and who wishes with all her heart to go to Him happens to commit a serious fault into which the demon makes the soul fall either by artfulness or by exertion, and which he fails not to augment as much as he possibly can; then taking the form and tone of an angel of light, he says to her in a severe and contemptuous manner, "How art thou fallen from heaven, then! who madest or rather flattered thyself that thou wouldst have become one of its most beautiful ornaments. Thou who saidst in thy heart: 'I will rise up, I will perfect myself, I will adorn my soul with all virtues, I will approach nearer and nearer to the Most High.' Behold then, thou art fallen into the abyss, rash spirit, audacious beginner who wished to soar rapidly up to the summit of perfection, and whose vain ambition and piety wanted to equal even the saints? What has become of your fine resolutions so often taken, repeated and written? Should this be the end of this original system of a refined devotion? *Do not raise your thoughts too high*," for he fears not to adopt the language of saints divinely inspired, in order to deceive the servants of God; he made use of them to God Himself to tempt Him in His human nature. "Learn," he says, "to humble yourself and follow the common way, vain and singular spirit. Notable examples of virtue are subjects of wonder, and not for your imitation."

There cannot be a more gross illusion: a beginner without

instruction as well as without experience can hardly be deceived by it. Does God laugh at a soul when she falls, and does He make her zeal and fervor subjects of reproach? Is it a crime to have wished to serve Him after we have offended Him? This does not require a long discussion. You ought then to arm yourself with strength, weak beginners, generous souls whose first steps in virtue are directed towards perfection. You ought to oppose truth to falsehood, and courage to temptations of fears, and answer the enemy thus: "Begone from me, Satan, or make use of other stratagems; your malice is misplaced.

"What I have to reproach myself with is not the sublimity of my views, and the austerity of my resolutions, but the inconstancy of my heart, and infidelity to my duties: 'tis not for having wished to love my God, because it was only for this reason that He created me, but to have attached myself to the creature which I should only have made use of to attain this end.

"Yes, I have wished to unite myself to my Creator who is the center as well as the principle of my being. I desire it more than ever, observing only to go to Him by the different degrees of a spiritual life, whether it is through weakness, malice, surprise, remainders of habit, or if it is by divine permission that I disillusion myself to render myself fit for solid virtue.

"I am fallen from it at present, but yet, I do not lose sight of it. The farther I have departed from it, the more I will redouble my efforts to approach it again. I do not affect extraordinary ways, I leave them for saints. But are not mortification of the senses, humility of heart, renouncing one self, obedience to my superiors, and deference to my equals, recollection and prayer, are not these the common way in which Christians are called to run with all their strength?

"You, my God, witness of my weakness and author of my resolutions, deign to affirm me. You know the desires of my heart; lead me to Yourself that my greatest consolation may be to imitate those souls who live only for You, that my sweetest moments may be those which I spend with You, and that I may tremble continually for the faults they may make me commit. My faults are great, indeed, but the pain I immediately feel on committing them convince me that I do not love them, and despite my infidelities, You still love me. Do not then abandon Your work, continue, hasten my sanctification. And since You *will* me also to work for it, I will renew my efforts with as much confidence, zeal and peace, as if I had never departed from it."

10.

Let us then conclude with St. Francis de Sales, a great saint whom I often quote. He is one of the greatest masters of spiritual life and interior peace: "You should, timid souls, look upon your faults with compassion rather than indignation, and with humility more than severity." Your sins can only astonish your presumption; reason ought rather to be surprised, and your piety be grateful towards God that you do not sin more. "You are not an impeccable God," says the pious and consoling a Kempis, "but a creature subject to sin; not a heavenly spirit but a man formed of clay and full of corruption."

Shall this clay and corruption be surprised to see a vapor of sin and a smell of death exhaling from it, from which neither the angels in heaven nor Adam in the terrestrial paradise were exempt? "I alone," says Our Lord, "am exempt from weakness and corruption; it is I who can support and deliver you from both, and who do it so far as to render partakers of my sanctity those souls who are well convinced of their misery and nothingness, who are entirely free from appropriating to themselves the merit of their own virtue and of depriving me of its glory."

Read this frequently, you whose sins commonly cast you into difficulty; read more often the *Spiritual Combat* by Lorenzo Scupoli. Above all, read the *Letters of Saint Francis de Sales* which breathe but peace and confidence, in the midst of our miseries. You cannot be too cautious in guarding against the trouble your sins occasion because presumption is commonly the most difficult to pacify, and the occasions of it are always inevitable in this life. The more surprised and troubled we will be at our faults, the more necessary they will be to us. God will permit them to cure us of our presumption. But when you will expect nothing from yourself but sin, even sin itself will not trouble you.

11.

Although I have already shown you not only the confidence, but even the simplicity with which you should return to God when you have strayed from sin, I cannot finish this chapter without speaking to you of simplicity in a more detailed manner. It is necessary to caution you against that rash haste which sometimes succeeds faint-heartedness and dejection. I repeat then that you should be as peaceable in your return from sin as you were patient in your fall; the one is almost inseparable from the other, and those who look upon their faults with more humility than vexation, grieve for them with more patience than activity.

The same pride which dismays and discourages the soul when it is dejected, inflames and transports it when it recovers what it had lost. In a moment, it passes from despair to presumption, and always by the same principle of self-confidence which is troubled and despairing when she sees herself confused, and proud and arrogant when she imagines she had the resources within her. Hope nothing from yourself, but hope all from God, repentance as well as pardon. Then, the desire and thought of returning to Him, and even your repentance will be simple, humble, discreet.

The prodigal son is the model of all true penitents. Behold him presenting himself before his father with a grave and serious, yet penitent and modest air. He does not strike his forehead, nor tear out his hair. Neither does the good he resolves upon for the future make him assume a firm and confident look. He ingenuously expresses the sentiments of his sorrow; he uses no lofty discourse to express his lively regret and sincere resolution. His countenance speaks for him; he omits half of the little he intended to say. As soon as the goodness of his father interrupts him when in tenderness he leans forward to kiss him, he does not by a mistaken humility draw back, nor do we observe in him a proud confidence.

The prodigal son allows himself to be stripped of his rags and to be clothed magnificently without breaking forth into unnecessary discourses. In humble silence, he beholds with grateful looks the feast which is being prepared for him. He takes his place at it, as soon as his father invites him, without exaggerating by misplaced exclamations his father's bounty and his own unworthiness. He does not listen to the concert in a melancholy and surprised manner; nor does he mix his voice with the music of the strangers. With a modest joy and a discreet reserve joined to sentiments of sorrow and gratitude which his full heart pours forth without affection, and with his eyes, he expresses the sincerity of his conversion and of true repentance.

Return to God then with more candor than activity. He is more pleased with an inflamed heart which cannot restrain the impetuosity of its effusions. If you think that your heart is in silence only because it is without fervor, offer it such as it is to God, beg Him to reanimate it, and do not prevent it by your own impatience; nor hinder by your own eagerness what God can do by His grace, and what He will do when He thinks proper.

CONCLUSION*

In Chapter VII of the original French text, the author cautions souls who love order and are profoundly interested in the glory of God, their eternal salvation, and the salvation of their fellow creatures not to concern themselves too much with the faults of others. This concern, if carried too far, might easily turn to wrath against someone, to impatience, indignation and disdain against him. Peace and charity must not be sacrificed in judgment of others.

What one does to oneself does not satisfy God's justice. The demon at work destroys one's interior peace which may affect one's health and disposition. Despite the passionate reaction against the faults of others, God is the example of patience, and justice should be left to Him.

Chapter VIII treats of moderation in all things, in our desires as well as our actions. This theme was treated in a previous chapter, but here in both desires and actions, we must first lift our spirit to God, to see His will in them, to act with reason, and not give way to whims. Not every desire or action we may have is praiseworthy, as mentioned in the *Imitation of Christ*. One must not follow impetuously even his best desires. Observe well whether they come from God or the demon, and choose only the *good*, acting peaceably, for the glory of God, in Him and by Him.

Chapters IX-XI treat of complete and universal detachment from all worldly goods and sensual pleasures in an effort to

---

* The conclusion of Part IV was left unfinished in Elizabeth Ann Seton's translation of this work. The Editor has attempted to group the main themes treated in Chapters VII-XI in a brief resumé.

acquire liberty of spirit and attain God. In desiring interior peace, the best and most effective means to obtain peace is to detach oneself from all creatures, and attach oneself only to God, to desire nothing that is not of God, nor for His glory and pleasure.

This detachment includes: too natural friendships that are not of God; detachment from oneself, one's curiosity, vanity, sloth, useless amusements, distracting friends with whom we are uncomfortable, all that nourishes self-love, and too great consolation taken from one's virtues, even in serving God with fidelity.

Complete detachment is not easily achieved, but by working continually, faithfully and courageously with an entire freedom of spirit, without constraint or fear, one strives to lose oneself in God, and thus gain our Heavenly Home.

* * * * *

Prayer to Obtain Interior Peace

All powerful God, You alone can restore peace in my heart; God of all goodness, with fidelity to your laws, You ask only for rest in our soul; Loving God, whose reign in us is but love and peace, fashion Yourself in my soul the silence for which You are waiting in order to communicate with it. I see in this soul only impatient eagerness, confusion, trouble.

Quiet action, desire without passion, zeal without agitation, can only come from eternal wisdom, infinite activity, unalterable rest which is the principle and model of real peace. It is so precious that Your love and generosity grant us Your peace in the next life, as the supreme recompense of the fidelity with which we shall have served You in this life. It is so delicate that it can only be perfected in heaven, and is so delicious that its enjoyment for all eternity cannot weary us.

Father of lights, it is from You alone, without change or vicissitudes that a gift so precious and perfect can descend upon us. You promised it through Your prophets, sent through Your Son, Jesus, confirmed through the Holy Spirit. Do not permit that the envy of our enemies, the trouble of our passions, the scruples of our conscience would cause us to lose this heavenly gift, which is the pledge of Your love, the object of Your promises and the price paid by the blood of Your Son, Jesus Christ. Amen.

S.M.C.

* * * * *

But your aridities call your attention to yourself in spite of yourself — yes and perhaps through self love more than through devotion — your pain is that you are displeased with yourself, and you think that it is because God is displeased with you — but if he chooses to conduct you by this way, why do you seek another? could the one you would choose please him better who asks nothing so much as submission to his will, or be more useful to you, who want nothing so much as to die to yourself — leave all to him — he knows better than you do what is best for you, Do your duty as perfectly as you can, and remain in peace — be contented with what he gives you, since he is willing to be content with what you are able to do for him —

8th. Life of faith.

Enter courageously in the life of faith in proportion to the measure with which God attracts you, and walk in it with freedom; never desiring to depart from it — let his obscurity be your light, and his firmness your support. the cloud of darkness will strike you with horror at first, your inquietude will be perpetual, you will desire like St Thomas to touch & to see, but if you faithfully resist, and resign yourself to see still less, instead of asking for light — if you shut your eyes to the false light of imagination which you are tempted to prefer to more useful darkness — and advance steadily in this obscurity where nothing rejoices your sight or consoles your heart but the accomplishment of Gods will, & the hope of his mercies an intimate and solid peace will be the fruit of your labour and

1. *Manuscripts of Saint Elizabeth Ann Seton*

The Book of Diaries
Books of Letters I-VI (chronological order)
The First Book of Instructions
The Second Book of Instructions
Books of Translations:
    Book I   The Life of Mr. Vincent
    Book II The Life of Madame Le Gras
               Excerpts from the Life of Ignatius of Loyola
    Book III Interior Peace by Ambroise de Lombez

Typescript copies of Elizabeth Ann Seton's manuscripts obtained from the Sacred Congregation for the Causes of the Saints in Rome were authenticated by the late Reverend Charles Léon Souvay, C.M. These are now preserved in the Archives of the Sisters of Charity at Seton Hill, Greensburg, Pennsylvania.

2. *Annotated Personal Books*

The Holy Bible. First American Edition. Philadelphia: Mathew Carey, 1805. Gift of Antonio Filicchi. Rare Books Collection at Notre Dame University, Indiana.

Commentary on the Book of Psalms by George, Lord Bishop of Norwich, Oxford, printed by William Young, Philadelphia, 1792. Gift of the Reverend John Henry

Hobart, June 17, 1802. Bruté Memorial Library, Vincennes, Indiana.

The Following of Christ by Thomas à Kempis. Translated into English by the Rt. Rev. Richard Challoner, D.D., Philadelphia: Mathew Carey, 1800. Archives of the Sisters of Charity, Seton Hill, Greensburg, Pennsylvania.

Prayer Book. No title or author; published before 1816. Robert Seton collection, Archives of Notre Dame University, Indiana. Gift of Bishop Cheverus of Boston.

3. French Books

The French books listed below were in Elizabeth Seton's possession at her death and were borrowed from the library of the Reverend Simon G. Bruté now preserved in the Bruté Memorial Library in Vincennes, Indiana.

(The asterisks indicate the books, portions of which Elizabeth Seton translated into English.)

Author not given. *Relation abrégée de la vie de Madame de Combé.* Institutrice de la Maison du Bon Pasteur. Paris: Florentin et Pierre Delaulne, 1700.

*Abelly, Louis (Evêque de Rodez). *La vie du vénérable serviteur de dieu, Vincent de Paul.* Paris: Florentin Lambert, 1664.

_____. *La conduite de l'église Catholique touchant le culte du très saint sacrement de l'Eucharistie.* Paris: Veuve Georges Jossé, 1678.

*Andilly, Arnauld d'. *Oeuvres de Sainte Thérèse.* Traduites en français par A. d'Andilly. Paris: Denys Thierry, 1687.

*Avrillon, Jean-Baptiste (Rev.). *Conduite pour passer saintement le temps de l'avent.* Marseille: Jean Mossy, 1811.

*Berthier, Guillaume-François (S.J.) *Les psaumes traduits en français avec des notes et des réflexions.* Paris: Adrien Le Clerc, 1807

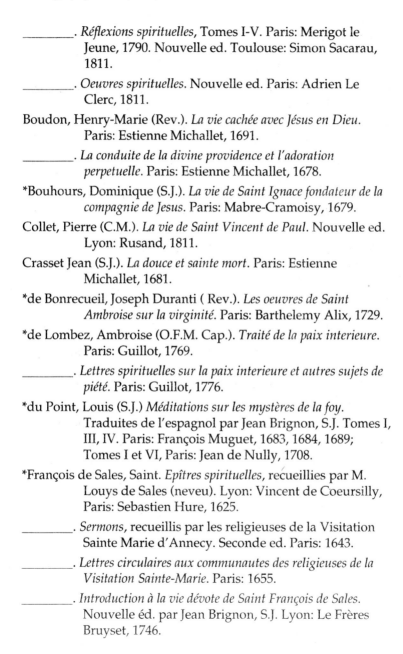

_____. *Réflexions spirituelles*, Tomes I-V. Paris: Merigot le Jeune, 1790. Nouvelle ed. Toulouse: Simon Sacarau, 1811.

_____. *Oeuvres spirituelles*. Nouvelle ed. Paris: Adrien Le Clerc, 1811.

Boudon, Henry-Marie (Rev.). *La vie cachée avec Jésus en Dieu.* Paris: Estienne Michallet, 1691.

_____. *La conduite de la divine providence et l'adoration perpetuelle.* Paris: Estienne Michallet, 1678.

*Bouhours, Dominique (S.J.). *La vie de Saint Ignace fondateur de la compagnie de Jesus.* Paris: Mabre-Cramoisy, 1679.

Collet, Pierre (C.M.). *La vie de Saint Vincent de Paul.* Nouvelle ed. Lyon: Rusand, 1811.

Crasset Jean (S.J.). *La douce et sainte mort.* Paris: Estienne Michallet, 1681.

*de Bonrecueil, Joseph Duranti (Rev.). *Les oeuvres de Saint Ambroise sur la virginité.* Paris: Barthelemy Alix, 1729.

*de Lombez, Ambroise (O.F.M. Cap.). *Traité de la paix interieure.* Paris: Guillot, 1769.

_____. *Lettres spirituelles sur la paix interieure et autres sujets de piété.* Paris: Guillot, 1776.

*du Point, Louis (S.J.) *Méditations sur les mystères de la foy.* Traduites de l'espagnol par Jean Brignon, S.J. Tomes I, III, IV. Paris: François Muguet, 1683, 1684, 1689; Tomes I et VI, Paris: Jean de Nully, 1708.

*François de Sales, Saint. *Epîtres spirituelles,* recueillies par M. Louys de Sales (neveu). Lyon: Vincent de Coeursilly, Paris: Sebastien Hure, 1625.

_____. *Sermons,* recueillis par les religieuses de la Visitation Sainte Marie d'Annecy. Seconde ed. Paris: 1643.

_____. *Lettres circulaires aux communautes des religieuses de la Visitation Sainte-Marie.* Paris: 1655.

_____. *Introduction à la vie dévote de Saint François de Sales.* Nouvelle éd. par Jean Brignon, S.J. Lyon: Le Frères Bruyset, 1746.

*Gobillon, Nicolas. *La vie de Mademoiselle Le Gras, fondatrice et première supérieure de la Compagnie des Filles de la Charité.* Paris: Pralard, 1676.

Huby, Vincent (S.J.). *Oeuvres spirituelles.* Paris: Gabrielle-Charles Berton, 1758.

Jegou, Jean (S.J.) *La préparation a la mort.* Rennes: François Vatar, 1688; Nicolas Devaux, 1733.

*Judde, Claude (S.J.) *Retraite spirituelle pour les personnes religieuses.* Paris: Gissey et Bordelet, 1746.

Lallemant, Louis (S.J.). *La doctrine spirituelle du Pere Louis Lallemant.* . . précédée de sa vie par Pierre Champion, S.J. Paris: Estienne Michallet, 1694.

La Valliere, Louise Françoise (Madame la duchesse de). *Réflexions sur la misericorde de Dieu.* Paris: Etienne-François Savoye, 1744.

Nicole, Pierre. *Essais de morale.* . . contenant des réflexions morales sur les Epîtres et Evangiles. Paris: Guillaume Desprez et Jean Dessartz, 1713.

Saint-Jure, Jean Baptiste (S.J.). *Meditations.* . . *de la foy.* Paris: Pierre le Petit, 1654.

_____. *Le Maistre Jésus Christ.* Paris: La Veuve Jean Camusat et Pierre le Petit, 1649.

_____. *Le livre des elus.* Paris: La Veuve Jean Camusat, 1643.

Surin, Jean-Joseph (S.J.). *Les fondements de la vie spirituelle tirés du livre de l'Imitation de Jésus-Christ.* Paris: Cramoisy, 1667, Nouvelle éd. revue et corrigée par Jean Brignon, S.J., 1703.

_____. *Dialogues spirituels choisis où la perfection chretienne est expliquée pour toutes les personnes.* Tome II. Troisieme éd. Paris: Edmé Couterot, 1719.

*Vincent de Paul, Saint. *Conférénces spirituelles pour l'explication des regles des Soeurs de Charite.* Paris: Demonville, 1803.

4. References

Books

Bruté, Rev. Simon G. *Mother Seton*, notes from the original papers in the possession of the Daughters of Charity Motherhouse, Emmitsburg, Maryland, 1884.

Bruté de Remur, Simon Guillaume Gabriel. *Selected Writings of Simon Gabriel Bruté*, edited by the Reverend Thomas G. Smith, S.T.D. Emmitsburg, Maryland: Mount Saint Mary's Seminary, 1977.

Celeste, Sister Marie, S.C. *Elizabeth Ann Seton: A Self-Portrait; A Study of Her Spirituality in Her Own Words*. Foreword by Bernard Basset, S.J. Libertyville, IL: Franciscan Marytown Press, 1986.

_____. *The Intimate Friendships of Elizabeth Ann Bayley Seton*. Foreword and Epilogue by David J. Hassel, S.J. Staten Island, New York: Alba House, 1989.

_____. *Elizabeth Ann Seton: A Woman of Prayer*. Foreword by Rev. Anselm W. Romb, O.F.M. Conv.; Staten Island, New York: Alba House, 1993.

Danemarie, Jeanne. *Une fille américaine de Monsieur Vincent*. Paris: Editions Spes, 1950.

De Barberey, Mme. Helene. *Elizabeth Seton*. Translated from the sixth French edition by the Rt. Rev. Msgr. Joseph B. Code, Emmitsburg, Maryland: Mother Seton Guild Press, 1957.

Seton, Rt. Rev. Robert. *Memoirs, Letters and Journal of Elizabeth Seton*. New York: P. O'Shea, 1896.

White, Charles I. (Rev.) *Life of Mrs. Eliza S. Seton*. New York: Edward Dunigan and Brother, 1853.